LOW CHOLESTEROL COOKBOOK FOR BEGINNERS

Transform Your Kitchen into a Sanctuary of Health
with Simple Yet Delectable Low Cholesterol Recipes Perfectly
Suited for Beginners

Laura L. Flores

Table of Contents

INTRODUCTION 5
   TYPES OF CHOLESTEROL 5
      HDL (High-Density Lipoprotein) – The Good Cholesterol 5
      LDL (Low-Density Lipoprotein) – The Bad Cholesterol 6
   RISKS OF HIGH CHOLESTEROL 6
   BENEFITS OF HDL 7
   HOW TODAY'S LIFE RHYTHMS LEAD TO POOR DIETS AND INITIATIVES TO RESOLVE THEM 8

FOODS TO AVOID 10
   CHOLESTEROL AND FATS 10
   TYPES OF FAT 11
      Trans Fats 11
   FOODS TO AVOID 12

PREFERRED FOODS ON LOW CHOLESTEROL DIET 14

SUPERFOODS AND SUPPLEMENTS TO LOWER CHOLESTEROL 17

BREAKFASTS RECIPES 19
   1. BREAKFAST QUINOA BOWL WITH MIXED FRUIT 20
   2. EGG WHITE FRITTATA WITH SPINACH, MUSHROOMS, AND FETA 20
   3. WHOLE GRAIN PANCAKES WITH BLUEBERRY COMPOTE 21
   4. GREEK YOGURT PARFAIT WITH FRESH BERRIES AND ALMONDS 21
   5. STEEL-CUT OATS WITH APPLE CINNAMON COMPOTE 22
   6. OATMEAL WITH BANANA AND WALNUTS 22
   7. BAKED EGG CUPS WITH SPINACH AND TOMATO 23
   8. FRUIT SALAD WITH COTTAGE CHEESE 23
   9. QUINOA BREAKFAST BOWL WITH SAUTÉED VEGETABLES AND EGG 24
   10. AVOCADO TOAST WITH POACHED EGGS 24

APPETIZERS RECIPES 25
   11. GRILLED EGGPLANT ROLLS WITH QUINOA AND PESTO 26
   12. CUCUMBER AND HUMMUS BITES 26
   13. BAKED SWEET POTATO FRIES WITH YOGURT DIP 27
   14. CAPRESE SKEWERS WITH CHERRY TOMATOES, MOZZARELLA, AND BASIL 27
   15. DEVILED EGGS WITH GREEK YOGURT AND DILL 28
   16. AVOCADO SHRIMP SALAD LETTUCE WRAPS 28
   17. TOFU SATAY SKEWERS WITH PEANUT SAUCE 29
   18. FRUIT SALSA WITH CINNAMON PITA CHIPS 29
   19. BEETROOT AND FETA BRUSCHETTA 30
   20. GREEK YOGURT DIP WITH FRESH VEGGIES 30
   21. GRILLED ZUCCHINI ROLLS WITH HERBED GOAT CHEESE 31

SNACKS RECIPES 32
   22. HOMEMADE GRANOLA BARS WITH OATS, NUTS, AND DRIED FRUIT 33
   23. CHIA SEED PUDDING WITH FRESH FRUIT TOPPING 33
   24. VEGAN SUSHI ROLLS WITH AVOCADO AND CUCUMBER 34
   25. SEAWEED SALAD WITH SESAME DRESSING 34
   26. TRAIL MIX WITH NUTS, SEEDS, AND DRIED FRUIT 35

27. Carrot Sticks with Hummus 35
28. Quinoa Salad Jars with Veggies and Lemon Herb Dressing 35
29. Apple Slices with Almond Butter 36
30. Cottage Cheese with Pineapple Chunks 36
31. Banana Chips 36

FIRST COURSES OF LAND 37

32. Whole Wheat Pasta Primavera with Roasted Vegetables 38
33. Spinach Salad with Strawberries and Almonds 38
34. Vegetable and Bean Chili 39
35. Lentil Soup with Vegetables 39
36. Minestrone Soup with Whole Wheat Pasta 40
37. Spaghetti Squash with Marinara Sauce 40
38. Cauliflower Fried Rice with Tofu 41
39. Tomato Basil Bruschetta 41
40. Stuffed Portobello Mushrooms with Quinoa and Spinach 42

SEAFOOD FIRST COURSES 43

41. Stuffed Squid with Quinoa and Spinach 44
42. Lemon Herb Baked Cod Fillets 44
43. Seafood Paella with Brown Rice 45
44. Salmon and Quinoa Salad with Lemon-Dill Dressing 45
45. Seafood Risotto with Asparagus and Peas 46
46. Seafood Salad with Greek Yogurt Dressing 47
47. Thai Coconut Curry Mussels 47
48. Cucumber and Smoked Salmon Roll-Ups 48
49. Grilled Shrimp Skewers with Pineapple and Bell Pepper 48
50. Shrimp and Vegetable Stir-Fry with Brown Rice 48
51. Baked Cod with Roasted Vegetables 49

SECOND COURSES OF LAND 50

52. Turkey Chili with Beans and Corn 51
53. Lemon Garlic Chicken Skewers 51
54. Grilled Steak Salad with Balsamic Vinaigrette 52
55. Chicken Piccata with Whole Wheat Pasta 52
56. Pan-Seared Duck Breast with Orange Glaze 53
57. Pork Stir-Fry with Snow Peas and Water Chestnuts 54

SEAFOOD SECOND COURSES 55

58. Baked Tilapia with Tomato and Herb Relish 56
59. Broiled Scallops with Garlic Butter 56
60. Seafood Paella with Shrimp, Mussels, and Clams 57
61. Grilled Lobster with Herb Butter 58
62. Grilled Swordfish with Mango Salsa 58
63. Pan-Seared Sea Bass with Lemon Caper Sauce 59
64. Baked Cod with Lemon and Herbs 59
65. Coconut Curry Shrimp with Rice Noodles 60
66. Baked Lemon Pepper Mahi Mahi 61
67. Lemon Herb Tilapia 61
68. Seared Scallops with White Wine Sauce 62

SIDE DISHES RECIPES 63

    69. Quinoa Pilaf with Vegetables 64
    70. Eggplant Caponata 64
    71. Asparagus Risotto with Parmesan Cheese 65
    72. Brown Rice with Peas and Carrots 65
    73. Sautéed Spinach with Garlic and Lemon 66
    74. Potato Leek Gratin with Gruyere Cheese 66
    75. Garlic Roasted Green Beans 67
    76. Grilled Corn on the Cob with Lime Cilantro Butter 67

SWEETS RECIPES 68

    77. Lemon Poppy Seed Muffins with Whole Wheat Flour 69
    78. Grilled Pineapple w/ Honey and Mint 69
    79. Baked Pear Crisp with Oat Topping 70
    80. Coconut Milk Rice Pudding with Mango 71
    81. Mango Sorbet 71
    82. Baked Apples with Cinnamon and Walnuts 72
    83. Dark Chocolate Covered Strawberries 72
    84. Berry Tart with Almond Flour Crust 73
    85. Avocado Chocolate Mousse 74
    86. Frozen Banana Bites with Peanut Butter 74

INSTANT POT RECIPES 75

    87. Black Bean and Sweet Potato Chili 76
    88. Stuffed Acorn Squash with Quinoa and Cranberries 76
    89. Chicken and Vegetable Paella 77
    90. Lentil and Vegetable Curry 78
    91. Ratatouille with Chickpeas 78
    92. Mediterranean Quinoa Salad 79
    93. Quinoa and Black Bean Stuffed Peppers 80

AIR FRYER RECIPES 81

    94. Harissa Spiced Chicken Thighs 82
    95. Air Fryer Veggie Tacos 82
    96. Ratatouille Stuffed Bell Peppers 83
    97. Roasted Brussels Sprouts with Balsamic Glaze 83
    98. Zucchini Chips with Herbed Yogurt Dip 84
    99. Baked Apples with Cinnamon 84
    100. Air Fryer Turkey Burgers 85
    101. Crispy Eggplant Parmesan 85
    102. Stuffed Bell Peppers with Quinoa and Black Beans 86

28 DAYS MEAL PLAN 87

    Daily List of Ingredients 90

CONVERSION CHART 106

CONCLUSION 107

INDEX 108

Introduction

Cholesterol is like a waxy material in your body. It's not necessarily bad because your body needs it to build cells and make certain important substances like vitamins and hormones. However, having too much of it can become a problem.

Your body gets cholesterol from two places. First, your liver produces all the cholesterol that your body needs. Second, you also get cholesterol from the foods you eat, especially from animal products like meat, poultry, and dairy.

Some foods that contain cholesterol also have unhealthy fats like saturated and trans fats. These fats can make your liver produce even more cholesterol than it should, leading to an unhealthy level of cholesterol in your body.

Certain oils like palm oil, palm kernel oil, and coconut oil, often used in baked goods, contain saturated fats that can raise bad cholesterol levels.

Cholesterol travels through your blood. When there's too much cholesterol in your blood, it can increase the risk of health problems like heart disease and stroke. That's why it's important to have your cholesterol checked regularly to know your levels.

There are 2 types of cholesterol: LDL (bad) and HDL (good). Having too much bad cholesterol or too little good cholesterol can lead to the buildup of cholesterol in the walls of your arteries, which can narrow them and make them less flexible. This condition is called atherosclerosis and can lead to heart attacks or strokes if a blood clot blocks a narrowed artery.

To manage cholesterol levels, it's important to remember three things: check, change, and control.

- Check your cholesterol levels regularly to assess your risk.
- Change your diet and lifestyle to improve your cholesterol levels, such as by eating healthier foods and exercising more.
- Control your cholesterol with the help of your doctor if needed, which may involve medication or other treatments.

High cholesterol is a significant risk factor for heart disease, heart attacks, and strokes. If you have other risk factors like smoking, high blood pressure, or diabetes, your risk is even higher. The more risk factors you have and the more severe they are, the greater your overall risk of these health problems.

Types of Cholesterol

Cholesterol, a lipid resembling wax, is present in every cell of the body and plays a vital role in bodily processes. Nevertheless, an extra of undesirable cholesterol can pose health risks. There exist two primary categories: low-density lipoprotein (LDL) and high-density lipoprotein (HDL).

HDL (High-Density Lipoprotein) – The Good Cholesterol

HDL, which stands for High-Density Lipoprotein, is often labeled as the "good" cholesterol because it plays a crucial role in maintaining our health. Unlike its counterpart, LDL (Low-Density Lipoprotein), which tends to accumulate in our arteries, causing potential blockages and heart-related issues, HDL works as a superhero in our bloodstream. Its primary job is to act like a scavenger, picking up extra cholesterol lingering in our blood vessels and shuttling it back to the liver for processing and eventual elimination from the body. This process is vital because it helps to clear out the "bad" cholesterol, also known as LDL, thus reducing the risk of heart disease and other cardiovascular problems.

Having high levels of HDL in our blood is highly beneficial for our overall health. It's like having a team of tiny cleaners constantly working to keep our arteries clear and our hearts strong. So, it's no surprise that healthcare professionals often emphasize the importance of maintaining optimal HDL levels.

Now, the question arises: how can we boost our HDL levels? Well, the good news is that there are several lifestyle changes we can make to enhance our HDL levels naturally. Regular physical activity, such as exercising or even just going for a brisk walk, can significantly raise HDL levels. Additionally, kicking unhealthy habits like smoking can also contribute to higher HDL levels. Furthermore, adopting a diet rich in healthy fats, such as those found in avocados, nuts, and olive oil, can further support HDL production.

In summary, when it comes to cholesterol, HDL is undoubtedly the superhero we want more of in our bloodstream. By taking proactive steps to boost our HDL levels through exercise, healthy eating, and lifestyle changes, we can promote heart health and overall well-being.

LDL (Low-Density Lipoprotein) – The Bad Cholesterol

LDL, short for Low-Density Lipoprotein, has earned its reputation as the "bad" cholesterol for good reason. Unlike its counterpart HDL, which acts as a guardian of our cardiovascular health, LDL can wreak havoc on our arteries and pose a significant risk to our heart health.

Imagine LDL as tiny, sticky particles that circulate in our bloodstream. When there's an extra of LDL, these particles tend to stick to the walls of our arteries, gradually building up and forming plaque. Over time, this plaque buildup can narrow our arteries, restricting blood flow to vital organs such as the heart and brain. This increases the risk of heart disease, heart attacks, and strokes.

While our bodies require some cholesterol to function properly, an abundance of LDL can be detrimental to our health. That's why it's crucial to keep LDL levels in check through various means. Adopting a healthy lifestyle, which includes regular exercise, maintaining a balanced diet low in saturated and trans fats, and avoiding smoking, can all help manage LDL levels.

In some cases, medication may also be prescribed to lower LDL levels, especially for individuals at high risk of heart disease or those who have difficulty managing their cholesterol through lifestyle changes alone. By taking proactive measures to control LDL levels, we can reduce the risk of heart disease and relish a healthier, happier life.

Risks of High Cholesterol

High cholesterol poses several risks to your health and well-being. When your body has an extra amount of cholesterol, it can build up in your arteries, leading to a condition called atherosclerosis. This buildup of cholesterol plaques can narrow your arteries and restrict blood flow to vital organs and tissues. Over time, this can contribute to various health problems, including heart disease, stroke, and peripheral artery disease.

One of the primary risks associated with high cholesterol is the development of heart disease. When cholesterol accumulates in the walls of your arteries, it can form plaque, which hardens and narrows the arteries. This condition, known as coronary artery disease, can restrict blood flow to the heart muscle, leading to chest pain (angina) or a heart attack. High levels of LDL cholesterol, often referred to as "bad" cholesterol, are particularly concerning in this regard, as they can increase the risk of plaque formation and heart disease.

Another significant risk of high cholesterol is the potential for stroke. If cholesterol plaques rupture or break off from artery walls, they can travel to smaller blood vessels in the brain, causing a blockage. This blockage can disrupt blood flow to parts of the brain, leading to a stroke. Depending on the severity and location of the blockage, a stroke can cause temporary or permanent damage, affecting various bodily functions, including movement, speech, and cognition.

Peripheral artery disease (PAD) is another consequence of high cholesterol. In PAD, cholesterol buildup narrows the arteries in the limbs, typically the legs. This can result in decreased blood flow to the legs and feet, leading to symptoms such as leg pain, numbness, and weakness, particularly during physical activity. In severe cases, PAD can cause tissue damage, non-healing wounds, and even limb amputation.

High cholesterol can also contribute to the formation of blood clots. When cholesterol plaques rupture, they expose the underlying tissue to the bloodstream, triggering the formation of blood clots. These clots can partially or entirely block blood flow, increasing the risk of heart attack or stroke.

Moreover, high cholesterol levels can impact other organs and systems in the body. For instance, cholesterol buildup in the blood vessels that supply the kidneys can lead to kidney disease or failure. Similarly, cholesterol deposits in the eyes can affect vision and increase the risk of conditions such as retinal artery occlusion.

In addition to the physical health risks, high cholesterol can also have psychological and emotional implications. Living with a chronic condition like high cholesterol may lead to increased stress, anxiety, or depression, particularly if it requires significant lifestyle changes or ongoing medical management.

The significance of maintaining healthy cholesterol levels is emphasized by the potential risks linked with high cholesterol. This can be achieved through lifestyle adjustments, including adopting a well-rounded diet, participating in consistent physical exercise, refraining from tobacco consumption, and addressing other risk factors like diabetes and obesity. In certain cases, healthcare professionals may also recommend medications, like statins, to aid in lowering cholesterol levels and mitigating associated complications. Regular monitoring and management of cholesterol levels are essential for preserving cardiovascular health and overall well-being.

Benefits of HDL

High-density lipoprotein (HDL) cholesterol is like the superhero of your body because it helps keep your heart healthy. Here's why it's so great:

- **Cleaning up cholesterol messes**: HDL takes the bad cholesterol (LDL) away from your arteries and brings it back to your liver where it's dealt with. This prevents LDL from clogging up your arteries and causing heart problems.
- **Fighting inflammation**: HDL can calm down inflammation, which is a big troublemaker for your heart. By reducing inflammation, HDL helps protect your heart from getting sick.
- **Shielding against damage**: HDL has special helpers that act like shields against harmful substances called oxidants. These shields protect your cells and tissues from damage, which is important for keeping your heart healthy.

- **Keeping blood vessels in shape**: HDL helps keep your blood vessels healthy and flexible. This is important because it helps regulate blood pressure and prevents blood clots from forming.
- **Cleaning up cholesterol messes, part 2**: HDL also helps get rid of extra cholesterol that's hanging around in your body. It takes this extra cholesterol back to your liver so it can be taken out, which helps keep your cholesterol levels in check and prevents artery blockages.
- **Protecting your heart**: Studies have found that people with higher levels of HDL cholesterol are less likely to have heart problems like heart attacks and strokes. So, having lots of HDL is like having a built-in shield for your heart.
- **Helping with blood sugar**: Some research suggests that HDL might help your body use insulin better and manage blood sugar levels. This is important because it can lower your risk of developing type 2 diabetes, which can lead to heart problems.

Keeping your HDL cholesterol levels high is really good for your heart. You can do this by staying active, eating healthy foods like fruits, veggies, and good fats, and avoiding smoking. But remember, your genes and overall health also play a role in your heart's health, so it's important to keep an eye on those too.

How Today's Life Rhythms Lead to Poor Diets and Initiatives to Resolve Them

In today's busy world, characterized by hectic schedules, demanding jobs, and constant connectivity, the rhythms of our lives have undergone significant shifts. Unfortunately, these changes often lead to detrimental dietary habits that contribute to poor health outcomes. Let's delve into some of the key factors contributing to this phenomenon:

1. **Busy Schedules**: Many people lead hectic lives with demanding work schedules, familial responsibilities, and social commitments. This often leaves little time for meal planning, cooking, and eating nutritious meals.
2. **Convenience Foods**: In our fast-paced world, convenience often takes precedence over nutrition. Processed and fast foods are readily available, affordable, and require minimal preparation time, making them a common choice for busy individuals.
3. **Stress**: Chronic stress can lead to emotional eating and cravings for high-fat, high-sugar comfort foods. Additionally, stress can disrupt hunger cues and lead to irregular eating patterns.
4. **Lack of Education**: Many people lack adequate knowledge about nutrition and healthy eating habits. Misinformation and conflicting dietary advice can further confuse individuals trying to make healthier choices.
5. **Food Marketing**: Aggressive marketing of unhealthy foods, especially to children and adolescents, can influence food choices and contribute to poor dietary habits.

To address these issues and promote healthier eating habits, several initiatives can be implemented:

1. **Nutrition Education Programs**: Schools, workplaces, and community centers can offer nutrition education programs to teach people about the importance of balanced diets, portion control, and reading food labels. These programs should be accessible and tailored to different age groups and socioeconomic backgrounds.

2. **Cooking Classes and Workshops**: Providing cooking classes and workshops can empower individuals to prepare healthy meals at home. These initiatives can teach basic cooking skills, recipe ideas, and budget-friendly meal planning tips.
3. **Promotion of Whole Foods**: Encouraging the consumption of whole, minimally processed foods can improve overall dietary quality. Initiatives such as farmers' markets, community gardens, and subsidies for fresh produce can increase access to nutritious foods.
4. **Policy Changes**: Governments can implement policies to regulate food marketing aimed at children, promote healthier food options in schools and workplaces, and incentivize food manufacturers to reduce the salt, sugar, and fat content of processed foods.
5. **Workplace Wellness Programs**: Employers can support employee health by offering wellness programs that include healthy eating initiatives, such as subsidized healthy food options, nutrition counseling, and onsite fitness facilities.
6. **Stress Management Strategies**: Teaching stress management techniques such as mindfulness, meditation, and regular physical activity can help individuals cope with stress without resorting to unhealthy eating habits.
7. **Community Support Networks**: Creating community support networks, such as cooking clubs, walking groups, or online forums, can provide social support and accountability for individuals striving to improve their diet and lifestyle.

By addressing the root causes of poor dietary habits and implementing initiatives that promote education, access to nutritious foods, and supportive environments, we can help individuals make healthier choices and improve overall public health.

Foods to Avoid

Maintaining healthy cholesterol levels is essential for overall well-being, and making mindful dietary choices plays a pivotal role in achieving this goal. By steering clear of certain foods, individuals can effectively manage their cholesterol levels and promote cardiovascular health.

Red meats, renowned for their high saturated fat content, are often best avoided by those seeking to regulate cholesterol levels. Similarly, organ meats, though rich in nutrients, can contribute to elevated cholesterol due to their high saturated fat content. Additionally, foods laden with saturated and trans fats, such as processed snacks and fried delights, should be consumed sparingly or substituted with healthier alternatives.

Understanding the body's natural cholesterol production process sheds light on the significance of dietary adjustments. Cholesterol, synthesized by the liver, serves as a fundamental component for cell membranes, facilitating essential cellular functions. Moreover, cholesterol plays a vital role in hormone synthesis, aids in the production of vitamin D, and supports the digestion of fatty foods.

However, an imbalance in cholesterol levels, influenced by lifestyle choices and genetic predispositions, can pose significant health risks. Excessive cholesterol accumulation in arterial walls hampers blood flow, heightening the risk of coronary heart disease, heart attacks, and strokes. Thus, adopting a wholesome, well-rounded diet emerges as a proactive approach to maintaining optimal cholesterol levels and safeguarding cardiovascular health.

By embracing a nutritious dietary regimen, individuals can mitigate the risk of cholesterol-related complications and foster overall well-being. Prioritizing whole grains, fruits, vegetables, and lean protein sources while limiting consumption of cholesterol-raising foods empowers individuals to take charge of their health and promote longevity. Moreover, complementing dietary modifications with regular exercise and other heart-healthy lifestyle practices further fortifies the body's defense against cholesterol-related ailments, fostering a vibrant and resilient cardiovascular system.

Cholesterol and Fats

Understanding the roles of cholesterol and fats in the body is pivotal for maintaining optimal health. Cholesterol, transported by two key proteins in the bloodstream – low-density lipoprotein (LDL) and high-density lipoprotein (HDL) – has a profound impact on cardiovascular health.

LDL, often termed "bad" cholesterol, has the tendency to deposit cholesterol in arteries, potentially leading to atherosclerosis and increasing the risk of heart disease and stroke. On the other hand, HDL, known as "good" cholesterol, plays a crucial role in removing extra LDL from arteries and transporting it to the liver for disposal, thereby mitigating cardiovascular risks.

Historically, dietary recommendations emphasized limiting cholesterol intake to 300 milligrams per day. However, recent research suggests that the cholesterol content of food has minimal impact on blood cholesterol levels for most people. Instead, emphasis has shifted towards prioritizing certain types of fats in the diet.

Both the American Heart Association (AHA) and the Centers for Disease Control and Prevention (CDC) advocate for prioritizing unsaturated fats, found in foods like nuts, seeds, avocados, and olive oil, over saturated and trans fats. Unsaturated fats have been associated with positive effects on cholesterol levels when consumed moderately, while saturated and trans fats, commonly found in processed and fried foods, are linked to elevated LDL cholesterol levels and increased cardiovascular risks.

Adopting a diet rich in unsaturated fats and limiting intake of saturated and trans fats can help manage blood cholesterol levels and reduce the risk of cardiovascular complications. However, individual dietary needs vary, and consulting with healthcare professionals or registered dietitians is crucial for personalized guidance on cholesterol management and overall dietary health.

Types of Fat

Types of fat play a crucial role in influencing cholesterol levels and overall cardiovascular health. Understanding the distinctions between various types of fat is essential for making informed dietary choices:

- **Saturated fats**: Predominantly found in animal products such as meat and dairy, saturated fats are known to prompt the liver to produce increased levels of LDL cholesterol ("bad cholesterol"). Excessive consumption of saturated fats is linked to heightened risks of heart disease and stroke.
- **Unsaturated fats**: Present in abundance in sources like fish, nuts, seeds, vegetable oils, and certain plant-based foods, unsaturated fats offer a healthier alternative to saturated fats. These fats can aid in enhancing the liver's capacity to reabsorb and break down LDL cholesterol, thus contributing to lower overall cholesterol levels. Incorporating unsaturated fats into one's diet can promote cardiovascular health and reduce the risk of chronic diseases.
- **Trans fats**: Often formed through the process of hydrogenation, trans fats are primarily found in solid vegetable oils. Commonly used in fried foods, baked goods, and various packaged products for their extended shelf life and texture enhancement, trans fats have adverse effects on cholesterol levels. Consumption of trans fats leads to elevated levels of LDL cholesterol while simultaneously reducing levels of HDL cholesterol, thereby increasing the risk of cardiovascular diseases and other health complications.

Individuals striving to maintain optimal cholesterol levels and promote heart health should prioritize the consumption of unsaturated fats while minimizing their intake of saturated and trans fats. By making mindful dietary choices and emphasizing healthier fat sources, individuals can effectively manage their cholesterol levels and reduce their susceptibility to cardiovascular diseases.

Trans Fats

Trans fats, scientifically referred to as trans fatty acids, are a type of unsaturated fat that can be harmful to health when consumed excessively. Unlike natural fats, trans fats are produced through an industrial process called hydrogenation, which involves adding hydrogen to liquid vegetable oils to make them more solid. This process is commonly used in food production to enhance the shelf life and texture of products.

Even though trans fats are beneficial in food production, they have been discovered to notably increase LDL (low-density lipoprotein) cholesterol, commonly referred to as "bad" cholesterol, while concurrently decreasing levels of HDL (high-density lipoprotein) cholesterol, known as "good" cholesterol. Elevated LDL cholesterol levels can accumulate within arteries, promoting atherosclerosis and heightening the likelihood of heart disease, whereas HDL cholesterol aids in removing LDL cholesterol from the bloodstream, thereby diminishing the risk of heart disease.

Extensive research on trans fat consumption consistently indicates its detrimental effects on cardiovascular health. For instance, a thorough literature review conducted in 2015 revealed a troubling link between trans fat intake and the risk of coronary heart disease. Even a slight increase in energy obtained from trans fats—just 2%—was associated with a significant 25% rise in the risk of coronary heart disease. Moreover, the risk of death from this condition increased by 31% with the same level of trans fat intake.

Furthermore, studies conducted in both the United States and China have identified alarming associations between higher trans fat consumption and increased rates of all-cause mortality, highlighting the widespread impact of trans fats on overall health and longevity.

In response to mounting concerns about the health risks posed by trans fats, several regions and countries have implemented bans or restrictions on their use in food production. Notably, New York enforced a ban on trans fats in foods in certain counties. A study conducted in 2017 examined the effects of this ban and found a significant reduction—6.2%—in hospital admissions for heart attacks and strokes in the affected counties. This evidence suggests that regulatory measures targeting trans fat content in foods can lead to tangible benefits for public health by decreasing the incidence of cardiovascular events.

While trans fats have been widely used in food manufacturing for their functional properties, their consumption presents significant health risks, particularly in terms of cardiovascular health. Research consistently links trans fat intake to elevated LDL cholesterol levels, an increased risk of heart disease, and higher mortality rates. Implementing policies to limit trans fat content in foods, as evidenced by the positive outcomes observed in regions with regulatory bans, is a critical step toward promoting public health and reducing the burden of cardiovascular diseases.

Foods to Avoid

To maintain a heart-healthy diet, it's crucial to adhere to recommendations regarding saturated fat intake, as advised by the American Heart Association (AHA). Limiting saturated fat to no more than 6% of total daily calorie intake is key. Here are some foods to avoid to achieve this goal:

- **Fatty Meats**: Steer clear of fatty cuts of beef, lamb, and pork, as they are high in saturated fat.
- **Poultry with Skin**: Take out the skin from poultry before consumption to reduce saturated fat intake.
- **Lard and Shortening**: These fats are rich in saturated fat and should be minimized in the diet.
- **Dairy Products**: Opt for skim or low-fat dairy options rather than whole or reduced-fat milk products to cut down on saturated fat intake.
- **Saturated Vegetable Oils**: Coconut oil, palm oil, and palm kernel oil are high in saturated fat and should be used sparingly.

In addition to limiting saturated fat, it's important to avoid trans fats, which can have detrimental effects on heart health. Here are some sources of trans fats to steer clear of:

- **Packaged Snacks**: Items like cookies, cakes, donuts, and pastries often contain trans fats and should be consumed sparingly.
- **Processed Foods**: Potato chips, crackers, and commercially fried foods are commonly made with trans fats and should be avoided or consumed in moderation.
- **Bakery Goods**: Be cautious of bakery items containing shortening, as they may contain trans fats.

- **Buttered Popcorn**: Popcorn prepared with butter may contain trans fats, so opt for air-popped or mildly seasoned varieties instead.
- **Hydrogenated Vegetable Oils**: Check food labels for partially hydrogenated or hydrogenated vegetable oils, as these contain trans fats and should be avoided.

When considering cholesterol intake, it's essential to be mindful of certain foods that are high in saturated fat and sodium. These include:

- **Red Meat**: Limit consumption of red meat, opting for lean cuts when possible.
- **Sausages and Bacon**: Processed meats like sausages and bacon are high in saturated fat and sodium and should be consumed in moderation.
- **Organ Meats**: Kidney and liver are high in cholesterol and saturated fat, so it's best to limit their intake.

By staying mindful of the foods you eat and opting for healthier options, you can lower the likelihood of heart disease and enhance your overall health.

Preferred Foods on Low Cholesterol Diet

What you eat affects your cholesterol. Some foods can raise it, while others can lower it. Keeping your cholesterol levels healthy can prevent health problems. Here are some foods that might help lower cholesterol when included in a balanced diet.

Eggplant

Eggplant is rich in dietary fiber, with 2.4 grams (g) per one-cup serving. According to the American Heart Association (AHA), fiber plays a crucial role in enhancing blood cholesterol levels and lowering the likelihood of various health conditions, including: Heart disease, Stroke, Obesity, Type 2 diabetes.

Okra

Okra, also known as lady's fingers, is a warm-flavour vegetable grown globally. Studies indicate that mucilage, a gel found in okra, can aid in reducing cholesterol levels by binding to it during the digestive process. Consequently, this facilitates the excretion of cholesterol through stool.

Apples

In a 2019 study involving 40 participants with mildly elevated cholesterol levels, the consumption of two apples per day resulted in reductions in both total and LDL cholesterol levels. Additionally, it led to decreased levels of triglycerides, a form of fat that enters the bloodstream post-meal.

A single apple can provide between 3 to 7 grams of dietary fiber, varying based on its size. Furthermore, apples contain polyphenols, compounds that may contribute to the beneficial impact on cholesterol levels.

Avocado

Avocados boast an abundance of heart-healthy nutrients. According to a 2015 study, incorporating one avocado daily into a moderate-fat, cholesterol-lowering diet can enhance cardiovascular health by reducing the risk of cardiovascular disease, notably by decreasing LDL cholesterol levels while preserving HDL cholesterol levels.

A single cup of avocado contains approximately 14.7 grams of monounsaturated fats, known to mitigate LDL cholesterol levels and diminish the likelihood of heart disease and strokes.

Fish

Omega-3 fats, including eicosapentaenoic acid (EPA), constitute vital polyunsaturated fats present in fish like salmon, mackerel, and sardines, renowned for their well-established anti-inflammatory properties and cardiovascular benefits.

EPA aids in safeguarding blood vessels and the heart from diseases by diminishing triglyceride levels. This mechanism stands as one among several ways EPA potentially averts atherosclerosis and mitigates the risk of cardiovascular ailments.

Moreover, EPA offers additional cardiovascular advantages, such as impeding the formation of cholesterol crystals within arteries, diminishing inflammation, and enhancing the functionality of HDL cholesterol.

Oats

In a small-scale 2017 study, oats demonstrated a substantial enhancement in blood cholesterol levels within a 4-week timeframe. The research team noted a notable reduction of 11.6% in LDL cholesterol levels among participants over the course of 28 days.

Further corroborating this finding, additional research from 2019 underscores the efficacy of the soluble fiber present in oats in lowering LDL cholesterol levels, thereby enhancing cardiovascular health as a component of a heart-healthy diet.

Individuals can simply incorporate oats into their daily diet regimen by consuming oatmeal or oat-based cereals for breakfast.

Barley

Barley, a nutritious grain abundant in vitamins, minerals, and fiber, offers numerous health benefits.

According to a 2020 study, the soluble fiber beta-glucan, present in barley, effectively lowers LDL cholesterol levels by capturing bile acids and restricting the amount of cholesterol immersed during digestion. As the body replenishes trapped bile acids by utilizing cholesterol, this process results in a general reduction in cholesterol levels.

Moreover, beta-glucan in barley exerts a positive influence on both the gut microbiome and blood sugar regulation, thereby contributing to overall heart health improvement.

Nuts

Nuts serve as an excellent source of unsaturated fats, known for their capacity to reduce LDL cholesterol levels, particularly when they replace saturated fats in one's diet. Additionally, nuts boast a rich fiber content, which aids in impeding cholesterol absorption and facilitating its elimination from the body.

All varieties of nuts are conducive to a heart-healthy, cholesterol-lowering diet, including: Almonds, Walnuts, Pistachios, Pecans, Hazelnuts, Brazil nuts, Cashews

Dark Chocolate

Cocoa, present in dark chocolate, harbors flavonoids, a class of compounds commonly found in numerous fruits and vegetables. These flavonoids possess antioxidant and anti-inflammatory characteristics that can confer various health benefits.

In a randomized trial conducted in 2015, participants consumed a cocoa flavanol-infused beverage twice daily for a month. At the conclusion of the trial, their LDL cholesterol levels and blood pressure had shown a decrease, while their HDL cholesterol levels had exhibited an increase.

Nevertheless, it's imperative for individuals to consume dark chocolate products judiciously, as they may contain elevated levels of saturated fats and sugar.

Lentils

Lentils boast a high fiber content, with approximately 7.8 grams per half-cup serving. Fiber plays a crucial role in preventing the absorption of cholesterol into the bloodstream.

In a small-scale 2015 study involving 39 participants diagnosed with type 2 diabetes and overweight or obesity, the consumption of lentil sprouts showcased favorable effects on cholesterol levels.

Garlic

Garlic is a versatile ingredient widely used in cooking, renowned for its numerous health benefits.

Studies have indicated that garlic possesses the ability to regulate serum cholesterol levels. Additionally, a meta-analysis conducted in 2015 concluded that garlic can contribute to lowering blood pressure.

It's worth noting that the reviews referenced primarily involved garlic supplements. Incorporating enough garlic into the diet to observe a significant impact on cholesterol levels might prove challenging.

Green tea

Certain teas, such as green tea, contain antioxidants known as catechins, which offer notable health benefits. In a review conducted in 2020, it was discovered that regular consumption of green tea led to significant improvements in cholesterol levels. Specifically, both total and LDL cholesterol levels were reduced without adversely affecting HDL cholesterol levels. However, the researchers emphasized the necessity for additional studies to validate and strengthen their findings.

Extra Virgin Olive Oil

Extra virgin olive oil is a staple ingredient in the heart-healthy Mediterranean diet, commonly employed as a cooking oil.

Replacing saturated fats with monounsaturated fats, abundant in extra virgin olive oil, may contribute to lowering LDL cholesterol levels.

Furthermore, extra virgin olive oil boasts antioxidant and anti-inflammatory properties that hold potential benefits for cardiovascular health and overall well-being.

Kale

Kale stands out as an exceptional source of fiber and numerous other essential nutrients. Just one cup of boiled kale offers 4.7 grams of fiber.

A review conducted in 2016 underscored the correlation between increased fiber intake and reductions in blood fat levels and blood pressure. Incorporating more fiber into the diet has been associated with decreased levels of total cholesterol and LDL cholesterol.

Additionally, kale is abundant in antioxidants, which play a pivotal role in promoting heart health and combating inflammation.

Superfoods and Supplements to Lower Cholesterol

Additional to exercise and dietary modifications, certain foods and supplements might aid in decreasing levels of low-density lipoprotein cholesterol.

If diagnosed with high cholesterol, physicians often prescribe statins, a medication aimed at reducing LDL cholesterol levels. Additionally, dietary adjustments and exercise enhancements may be recommended. Dietary modifications may involve incorporating cholesterol-lowering foods.

The desirable cholesterol levels are as follows:

- Total cholesterol: less than 200 milligrams per deciliter (mg/dL)
- LDL cholesterol: less than 100 mg/dL
- HDL cholesterol: 60 mg/dL or higher

Factors such as being overweight or leading a sedentary lifestyle may increase the risk of high LDL cholesterol. Genetic predisposition can also contribute to elevated cholesterol levels.

Cholesterol is synthesized by the liver and can be obtained from certain food sources, although not to the same extent as from foods rich in saturated and trans fats. Consumption of these fats prompts the liver to produce extra cholesterol.

However, there are dietary options and supplements derived from food sources that can also aid in lowering cholesterol levels.

Niacin

Niacin, a B vitamin, is occasionally recommended by doctors for individuals with elevated cholesterol levels or cardiovascular issues. It promotes an increase in high-density lipoprotein (HDL) cholesterol levels and decreases triglycerides, an additional type of fat that can contribute to arterial blockages. Niacin can be obtained from dietary sources, particularly liver and chicken, or through supplements.

The suggested daily niacin intake is 14 milligrams for women and 16 milligrams for men. However, it is crucial not to take supplements without the guidance of a healthcare professional. Ingesting niacin supplements without proper recommendation can lead to adverse effects such as skin itching, flushing, nausea, and more.

Soluble Fiber

There exist two varieties of fiber: soluble, which forms a gel-like substance when mixed with liquid, and insoluble. Soluble fiber functions to reduce the absorption of cholesterol in the bloodstream. The suggested daily fiber consumption differs according to age and gender:

- Men aged 50 and under: 38 grams - Men over 50: 30 grams
- Women aged 50 and under: 25 grams - Women over 50: 21 grams

The good news is that soluble fiber can be found in foods you likely already relish: Orange: 1.8 grams, Pear: 1.1 to 1.5 grams, Peach: 1.0 to 1.3 grams, Asparagus (1/2 cup): 1.7 grams, Potato: 1.1 grams, Whole wheat bread (1 slice): 0.5 grams, Oatmeal (1 1/2 cups): 2.8 grams, Kidney beans (175 milliliters, approximately 3/4 cup): 2.6 to 3 grams

Psyllium Supplements

Psyllium is a type of fiber derived from the husks of seeds from the Plantago ovata plant. It can be consumed in pill form or added to drinks or food.

Regular intake of psyllium has been demonstrated to notably decrease cholesterol levels. Additionally, it provides relief from constipation and may help in lowering blood sugar levels for individuals with diabetes.

Phytosterols

Phytosterols, derived from plants, are waxy substances that hinder the absorption of cholesterol in the intestines. They are naturally found in whole grains, nuts, fruits, and vegetables.

Food producers have started incorporating phytosterols into various prepared foods, including margarine and yogurt. This means that you can consume foods containing cholesterol and simultaneously counteract some of its effects by ingesting phytosterols.

Soy Protein

Soybeans and soy-based products like tofu, soy milk, and soy yogurt are recommended for inclusion in a diet aimed at lowering cholesterol levels.

A comprehensive 2019 analysis, comprising 46 studies investigating the impact of soy on LDL cholesterol, revealed that a median daily intake of 25 grams of soy protein over a period of 6 weeks resulted in a clinically significant reduction of 4.76 milligrams per deciliter in LDL cholesterol levels.

The collective findings of these studies led the researchers to conclude that soy protein intake can contribute to a 3–4% reduction in LDL cholesterol levels among adults, solidifying its role in promoting heart health and supporting a cholesterol-lowering diet.

Red Yeast Rice

Red yeast rice is a type of white rice that undergoes fermentation with yeast, commonly consumed and utilized as a medicinal remedy in China.

Certain red yeast rice supplements have demonstrated cholesterol-lowering effects due to the presence of monacolin K, which shares a similar chemical composition with lovastatin, a medication used to reduce cholesterol levels.

However, in the United States, red yeast rice supplements do not contain monacolin K. This is because the FDA determined in 1998 that monacolin K qualified as a medication and could not be marketed as a dietary supplement.

Although red yeast rice supplements are still available, they do not include monacolin K. Additionally, it's important to note that red yeast rice may potentially induce kidney, liver, and muscle damage.

Ginger

A study conducted in 2014 indicated that ginger has the potential to decrease total cholesterol and triglyceride levels. Additionally, a study from 2008 demonstrated its ability to reduce LDL cholesterol levels and increase HDL cholesterol levels.

Ginger can be incorporated into meals in its raw form or consumed as a supplement or powder.

Flaxseed

Flax, a blue flower cultivated in temperate climates, yields seeds and oil rich in omega-3 fatty acids, offering various health benefits, such as increasing HDL cholesterol levels.

For optimal health benefits from flaxseed, it's recommended to consume its oil or ground form rather than whole seeds. This is because our bodies cannot digest the shiny outer shell of the seed.

Breakfasts Recipes

1. Breakfast Quinoa Bowl with Mixed Fruit

Recipe type:
Difficulty: Easy · **Preparation time:** 10 minutes
Cooking time: 15 minutes · **Servings:** 2
Ingredients:

- 1/2 cup quinoa, washed
- 1 cup water or milk
- 1/2 tsp. cinnamon
- 1 ripe banana, cut
- 1/2 cup mixed fresh fruit (e.g., berries, kiwi, mango)
- 2 tbsps. chopped nuts (e.g., almonds, walnuts)
- Optional: honey or maple syrup for sweetness

Directions:

1. In your small saucepan, bring the water or milk to a boil.
2. Put the quinoa and cinnamon, then decrease the temp. to low.
3. Cover then simmer for around 15 minutes, or 'til the quinoa is cooked and the liquid is immersed.
4. Fluff the quinoa using a fork and split it between two serving bowls.
5. Top all bowls with cut banana, mixed fresh fruit, and chopped nuts.
6. Drizzle using honey or maple syrup if wanted.
7. Present hot.

Per serving: Calories: 306kcal; Fat: 7g; Carbs: 55g; Protein: 9g; Sugar: 16g; Sodium: 10mg; Potassium: 472mg; Glycemic index: 45

2. Egg White Frittata with Spinach, Mushrooms, and Feta

Recipe type:
Difficulty: Medium · **Preparation time:** 10 minutes
Cooking time: 20 minutes · **Servings:** 2
Ingredients:

- 6 egg whites
- 1 cup spinach leaves, chopped
- 1/2 cup cut mushrooms
- 1/4 cup crumbled feta cheese
- 1 tbsp. olive oil
- Salt and pepper as required

Directions:

1. Warm up the oven to 350 deg.F.
2. In your mixing bowl, whisk the egg whites 'til frothy. Flavour using salt and pepper.
3. Warm olive oil in an oven-safe skillet in a middling temp.
4. Include chopped spinach then cut mushrooms to your skillet. Sauté 'til the vegetables are wilted and any extra moisture has evaporated (3-5 minutes).
5. Put the whisked egg whites over the sautéed vegetables in the skillet.
6. Cook without mixing 'til the edges start to set, about 2-3 minutes.
7. Sprinkle your crumbled feta cheese uniformly over the top of the frittata.
8. Put the skillet to your warmed up oven then bake for 10-12 minutes, or 'til the frittata is set in the center and mildly golden on top.
9. Take out from the oven then let it cool for a couple of minutes prior to cutting.
10. Present warm.

Per serving: Calories: 169kcal; Fat: 9g; Carbs: 5g; Protein: 16g; Sugar: 2g; Sodium: 450mg; Potassium: 346mg; Glycemic index: 15

3. Whole Grain Pancakes with Blueberry Compote

Recipe type:
Difficulty: Easy · **Preparation time:** 10 minutes
Cooking time: 10 minutes · **Servings:** 2
Ingredients:

- 1 cup whole wheat flour
- 1 tbsp. baking powder
- 1 tbsp. honey or maple syrup
- 1 cup milk of your choice
- 1 big egg
- 1 cup fresh or frozen blueberries
- Optional: additional honey or maple syrup for presenting

Directions:

1. In the mixing bowl, blend the whole wheat flour, baking powder, honey or maple syrup, milk, and egg. Mix 'til smooth.
2. Warm a non-stick skillet or griddle in a middling temp.
3. Put a ladleful of pancake batter onto your skillet for all pancakes.
4. Cook 'til bubbles appear on the surface, then flip then cook 'til golden brown on both sides.
5. In your small saucepan, heat the blueberries in a middling temp. 'til they start to release their juices and soften, around 5 minutes.
6. Mash the blueberries mildly using a fork to create a compote consistency.
7. Present the pancakes with the blueberry compote on top.
8. Drizzle using additional honey or maple syrup if wanted and present hot.

Per serving: Calories: 378kcal; Fat: 6g; Carbs: 72g; Protein: 14g; Sugar: 26g; Sodium: 520mg; Potassium: 607mg; Glycemic index: 50

4. Greek Yogurt Parfait with Fresh Berries and Almonds

Recipe type:
Difficulty: Easy
Preparation time: 5 minutes
Cooking time: 0 minutes
Servings: 2
Ingredients:

- 1 cup plain Greek yogurt
- 1/2 cup fresh berries (e.g., strawberries, blueberries, raspberries)
- 1/4 cup cut almonds
- 1 tbsp. honey (optional)

Directions:

1. In two serving glasses or bowls, layer the Greek yogurt, fresh berries, then cut almonds.
2. Repeat the layers 'til the glasses are filled.
3. Drizzle honey over the top if wanted.
4. Present instantly.

Per serving: Calories: 210kcal; Fat: 9g; Carbs: 18g; Protein: 17g; Sugar: 10g; Sodium: 48mg; Potassium: 269mg; Glycemic index: 25

5. Steel-Cut Oats with Apple Cinnamon Compote

Recipe type:
Difficulty: Medium · **Preparation time:** 5 minutes
Cooking time: 30 minutes · **Servings:** 2
Ingredients:

- 1/2 cup steel-cut oats
- 2 cups water or almond milk
- 2 medium apples, skinned, cored, and diced
- 1 tbsp. maple syrup or honey
- 1 tsp. ground cinnamon
- Pinch of salt
- Optional toppings: chopped nuts, raisins, additional maple syrup

Directions:

1. In your saucepan, bring the water or almond milk to a boil.
2. Stir in the steel-cut oats then decrease the temp. to low.
3. Simmer, uncovered, mixing irregularly, 20-30 minutes, or 'til the oats are tender and creamy.
4. In your distinct saucepan, blend the diced apples, maple syrup or honey, ground cinnamon, and a pinch of salt.
5. Cook in a middling temp., mixing irregularly, 'til the apples are softened then the mixture has thickened into a compote consistency, around 10-15 minutes.
6. Present the cooked steel-cut oats topped with the apple cinnamon compote.
7. Garnish using chopped nuts, raisins, or a drizzle of additional maple syrup if wanted.
8. Present hot.

Per serving: Calories: 280kcal; Fat: 2g; Carbs: 61g; Protein: 6g; Sugar: 26g; Sodium: 150mg; Potassium: 430mg; Glycemic index: 40

6. Oatmeal with Banana and Walnuts

Recipe type:
Difficulty: Easy · **Preparation time:** 5 minutes
Cooking time: 5 minutes · **Servings:** 2
Ingredients:

- 1 cup old-fashioned oats
- 2 cups water or milk
- 1 ripe banana, cut
- 1/4 cup chopped walnuts
- Optional: honey or maple syrup for sweetness

Directions:

1. In your saucepan, bring the water or milk to a boil.
2. Stir in the oats then decrease the temp. to low.
3. Cook oats using the package guidelines, usually around 5 minutes, mixing irregularly.
4. Once oatmeal reaches your desired consistency, take out from heat.
5. Split the cooked oatmeal between two bowls.
6. Top all bowls with cut banana and chopped walnuts.
7. Drizzle using honey or maple syrup if wanted.
8. Present hot.

Per serving: Calories: 312kcal; Fat: 10g; Carbs: 52g; Protein: 9g; Sugar: 14g; Sodium: 10mg; Potassium: 490mg; Glycemic index: 50

7. Baked Egg Cups with Spinach and Tomato

Recipe type:
Difficulty: Hard
Preparation time: 15 minutes
Cooking time: 25 minutes
Servings: 2
Ingredients:

- 4 big eggs
- 1 cup fresh spinach leaves, chopped
- 1/2 cup diced tomatoes
- 1/4 cup shredded cheese (any variety)
- Salt and pepper as required
- Olive oil or cooking spray

Directions:

1. Warm up the oven to 375 deg.F. Grease a muffin tin using olive oil or cooking spray.
2. In your mixing bowl, beat the eggs 'til well blended. Flavour using salt and pepper.
3. Split the chopped spinach and diced tomatoes uniformly among the muffin cups.
4. Place beaten eggs over the spinach and tomatoes, filling each muffin cup around 3/4 full.
5. Sprinkle shredded cheese over the top of each egg cup.
6. Bake in to your warmed up oven for 20-25 minutes, or 'til the egg cups are set and mildly golden on top.
7. Take out from the oven then let them cool mildly prior to presenting.
8. Present warm.

Per serving: Calories: 220kcal; Fat: 14g; Carbs: 6g; Protein: 16g; Sugar: 3g; Sodium: 320mg; Potassium: 430mg; Glycemic index: 20

8. Fruit Salad with Cottage Cheese

Recipe type:
Difficulty: Easy
Preparation time: 10 minutes
Cooking time: 0 minutes
Servings: 2
Ingredients:

- 1 cup cottage cheese
- 1 cup mixed fresh fruits (e.g., strawberries, pineapple, grapes, kiwi)
- Optional: mint leaves for garnish

Directions:

1. Wash and prepare the fruits as needed. Cut them into bite-sized pieces if necessary.
2. Split the cottage cheese equally between two serving bowls.
3. Organize the mixed fruits on top of the cottage cheese.
4. Garnish using mint leaves if wanted.
5. Present instantly.

Per serving: Calories: 196kcal; Fat: 6g; Carbs: 20g; Protein: 16g; Sugar: 16g; Sodium: 576mg; Potassium: 274mg; Glycemic index: 45

9. Quinoa Breakfast Bowl with Sautéed Vegetables and Egg

Recipe type:
Difficulty: Medium · **Preparation time:** 10 minutes
Cooking time: 20 minutes · **Servings:** 2
Ingredients:

- 1/2 cup quinoa, washed
- 1 cup water or vegetable broth
- 1 tbsp. olive oil
- 1/2 cup diced bell peppers
- 1/2 cup diced zucchini
- 1/4 cup diced onion
- 2 pieces garlic, crushed
- 2 big eggs
- Salt and pepper as required
- Optional: chopped parsley for garnish

Directions:

1. In your saucepan, bring the water or vegetable broth to a boil. Put the quinoa, then decrease the temp. to low. Cover then simmer for around 15-20 minutes, or 'til the quinoa is cooked and the liquid is immersed.
2. Warm olive oil in your skillet in a middling temp. Put the diced bell peppers, zucchini, onion, and crushed garlic. Sauté 'til the vegetables are tender, around 5-7 minutes.
3. In your distinct non-stick skillet, cook the eggs to your desired level of doneness (fried, poached, or scrambled).
4. To manufacture the bowls, split the cooked quinoa between two serving bowls. Top with the sautéed vegetables then cooked eggs.
5. Flavour using salt and pepper as required.
6. Garnish using chopped parsley if wanted.
7. Present hot.

Per serving: Calories: 320kcal; Fat: 14g; Carbs: 37g; Protein: 14g; Sugar: 5g; Sodium: 80mg; Potassium: 616mg; Glycemic index: 45

10. Avocado Toast with Poached Eggs

Recipe type:
Difficulty: Easy
Preparation time: 10 minutes
Cooking time: 5 minutes
Servings: 2
Ingredients:

- 2 slices whole wheat bread
- 1 ripe avocado
- 2 big eggs
- Salt and pepper as required

Directions:

1. Toast the whole wheat bread slices 'til golden brown.
2. While bread is toasting, slice the avocado and mash it using a fork in a small bowl. Flavour using salt and pepper.
3. Poach eggs to your desired level of doneness.
4. Disperse mashed avocado uniformly onto the toasted bread slices.
5. Carefully put a poached egg on top of each avocado toast.
6. Flavour eggs using additional salt and pepper if wanted.
7. Present instantly.

Per serving: Calories: 270kcal; Fat: 15g; Carbs: 23g; Protein: 12g; Sugar: 2g; Sodium: 205mg; Potassium: 522mg; Glycemic index: 15

Appetizers Recipes

11. Grilled Eggplant Rolls with Quinoa and Pesto

Recipe type:
Difficulty: Hard
Preparation time: 30 minutes
Cooking time: 15 minutes
Servings: 2 (8 rolls)
Ingredients:

- 1 big eggplant, finely cut lengthwise
- 1 cup cooked quinoa
- 1/4 cup pesto sauce
- 2 tbsps. chopped fresh basil
- 2 tbsps. pine nuts, toasted
- 1 tbsp. olive oil
- Salt and pepper as required

Directions:

1. Warm up a grill pan in a med-high temp.
2. Brush both sides of your eggplant slices using olive oil and flavour using salt and pepper.
3. Grill eggplant slices for 2-3 minutes on all sides, or 'til tender and grill marks appear.
4. In your mixing bowl, blend cooked quinoa, pesto sauce, chopped fresh basil, and toasted pine nuts. Stir 'til well blended.
5. Put a spoonful of the quinoa mixture on one end of each grilled eggplant slice.
6. Roll up the eggplant slices with the quinoa filling.
7. Secure the rolls with toothpicks if necessary.
8. Present the grilled eggplant rolls warm or at room temp.

Per serving: Calories: 280kcal; Fat: 16g; Carbs: 30g; Protein: 7g; Sugar: 3g; Sodium: 380mg; Potassium: 750mg; Glycemic index: 15

12. Cucumber and Hummus Bites

Recipe type:
Difficulty: Easy
Preparation time: 10 minutes
Cooking time: 0 minutes
Servings: 2 (8 bites)
Ingredients:

- 1 big cucumber
- 1/2 cup hummus
- Paprika or cayenne pepper, for garnish (optional)
- Fresh parsley or dill, for garnish (optional)

Directions:

1. Wash the cucumber then slice it into rounds, around 1/2-inch dense.
2. Spoon a small dollop of hummus onto each cucumber round.
3. Sprinkle using paprika or cayenne pepper for a touch of heat, if wanted.
4. Garnish using fresh parsley or dill for added flavor, if wanted.
5. Organize the cucumber and hummus bites on your serving platter.
6. Present instantly.

Per serving: Calories: 80kcal; Fat: 4g; Carbs: 9g; Protein: 4g; Sugar: 2g; Sodium: 160mg; Potassium: 320mg; Glycemic index: 15

13. Baked Sweet Potato Fries with Yogurt Dip

Recipe type:

Difficulty: Medium · **Preparation time:** 15 minutes

Cooking time: 25 minutes · **Servings:** 2

Ingredients:

For the sweet potato fries:

- 2 medium sweet potatoes, cut into fries
- 1 tbsp. olive oil
- 1/2 tsp. paprika
- 1/2 tsp. garlic powder
- Salt and pepper as required

For the yogurt dip:

- 1/2 cup Greek yogurt
- 1 tbsp. lemon juice
- 1 clove garlic, crushed
- 1 tbsp. chopped fresh dill
- Salt and pepper as required

Directions:

1. Warm up the oven to 425 deg.F. Cover a baking sheet with parchment paper and put it away.
2. In your mixing bowl, toss the sweet potato fries with salt, olive oil, paprika, garlic powder, and pepper 'til uniformly covered.
3. Organize sweet potato fries in a one layer on your organized baking sheet.
4. Bake in to your warmed up oven for 20-25 minutes, turning them over on the halfway point, 'til golden brown and crispy.
5. While sweet potato fries are baking, prepare the yogurt dip. In your small bowl, blend the Greek yogurt, lemon juice, crushed garlic, chopped fresh dill, salt, and pepper. Stir 'til well blended.
6. Once the sweet potato fries are done baking, take them out from the oven then let them cool mildly.
7. Present the sweet potato fries with the yogurt dip on the side.

Per serving: Calories: 250kcal; Fat: 7g; Carbs: 41g; Protein: 7g; Sugar: 10g; Sodium: 280mg; Potassium: 750mg; Glycemic index: 50

14. Caprese Skewers with Cherry Tomatoes, Mozzarella, and Basil

Recipe type:

Difficulty: Easy

Preparation time: 10 minutes

Cooking time: 0 minutes

Servings: 2 (6 skewers)

Ingredients:

- 12 cherry tomatoes
- 6 small fresh mozzarella balls (bocconcini)
- 12 fresh basil leaves
- Balsamic glaze, for drizzling (optional)
- Salt and pepper as required
- Wooden skewers

Directions:

1. Rinse the cherry tomatoes then pat them dry using a paper towel.
2. Thread a cherry tomato onto a wooden skewer, followed by a mozzarella ball and your basil leaf.
3. Repeat the process 'til each skewer has two cherry tomatoes, one mozzarella ball, and two basil leaves.
4. Organize the skewers on your serving platter.
5. Drizzle using balsamic glaze if wanted.
6. Flavour using salt and pepper as required.
7. Present instantly.

Per serving: Calories: 120kcal; Fat: 7g; Carbs: 5g; Protein: 8g; Sugar: 2g; Sodium: 240mg; Potassium: 200mg; Glycemic index: 15

15. Deviled Eggs with Greek Yogurt and Dill

Recipe type:

Difficulty: Easy · **Preparation time:** 15 minutes

Cooking time: 10 minutes · **Servings:** 2 (6 deviled egg halves)

Ingredients:

- 3 big eggs
- 2 tbsps. Greek yogurt
- 1 tsp. Dijon mustard
- 1 tsp. lemon juice
- 1 tsp. chopped fresh dill
- Salt and pepper as required
- Paprika or chopped chives for garnish (optional)

Directions:

1. Put eggs in your saucepan and cover with water. Bring to a boil in a med-high temp.
2. Once boiling, decrease the temp. to low then let the eggs simmer for 10 minutes.
3. Take out the eggs from the saucepan and put them in a bowl of ice water to cool.
4. Once cooled, carefully peel the eggs then slice them in half lengthwise. Take out the yolks and put them in a distinct bowl.
5. Mash the egg yolks using a fork 'til smooth.
6. Put the Greek yogurt, Dijon mustard, lemon juice, chopped dill, salt, and pepper to the mashed egg yolks. Mix 'til well blended.
7. Spoon or pipe yolk mixture back into your egg white halves.
8. Garnish using a sprinkle of paprika or chopped chives, if wanted.
9. Present chilled.

Per serving: Calories: 110kcal; Fat: 7g; Carbs: 2g; Protein: 9g; Sugar: 1g; Sodium: 140mg; Potassium: 120mg; Glycemic index: 0

16. Avocado Shrimp Salad Lettuce Wraps

Recipe type:

Difficulty: Medium · **Preparation time:** 15 minutes

Cooking time: 5 minutes · **Servings:** 2 (4 lettuce wraps)

Ingredients:

- 8 big cooked shrimp, skinned and deveined
- 1 ripe avocado, diced
- 1/4 cup diced cucumber
- 1/4 cup diced red bell pepper
- 2 tbsps. chopped fresh cilantro
- 1 tbsp. lime juice
- Salt and pepper as required
- 4 big lettuce leaves (e.g., romaine or butter lettuce)

Directions:

1. In your mixing bowl, blend the cooked shrimp, diced avocado, diced cucumber, diced red bell pepper, chopped fresh cilantro, and lime juice.
2. Gently toss 'til well blended.
3. Flavour using salt and pepper as required.
4. Split the shrimp salad uniformly among the lettuce leaves.
5. Wrap the lettuce leaves around the shrimp salad to form wraps.
6. Present instantly.

Per serving: Calories: 160kcal; Fat: 9g; Carbs: 12g; Protein: 10g; Sugar: 2g; Sodium: 200mg; Potassium: 480mg; Glycemic index: 15

17. Tofu Satay Skewers with Peanut Sauce

Recipe type:

Difficulty: Hard · **Preparation time:** 30 minutes
Cooking time: 15 minutes · **Servings:** 2
Ingredients:

For the tofu satay skewers:

- 8 oz firm tofu, cut into cubes
- 2 tbsps. soy sauce
- 1 tbsp. lime juice
- 1 tbsp. maple syrup
- 1 clove garlic, crushed
- 1 tsp. grated ginger
- 1/2 tsp. ground cumin
- 1/2 tsp. ground coriander
- 1/4 tsp. turmeric
- 8 bamboo skewers, soaked in a water for 30 minutes

For the peanut sauce:

- 1/4 cup peanut butter
- 2 tbsps. soy sauce
- 1 tbsp. lime juice
- 1 tbsp. maple syrup
- 1 tsp. grated ginger
- 1 clove garlic, crushed
- Water, as needed to thin the sauce

Directions:

1. In your shallow dish, whisk collectively soy sauce, lime juice, maple syrup, crushed garlic, grated ginger, ground cumin, ground coriander, and turmeric.
2. Put the tofu cubes to the marinade then toss 'til well coated. Let marinate for almost 15 minutes.
3. While tofu is marinating, prepare the peanut sauce. In your small saucepan, blend peanut butter, soy sauce, lime juice, maple syrup, crushed garlic, grated ginger, then cook over low heat, mixing regularly 'til smooth. If sauce is too dense, include water gradually 'til desired consistency is reached. Take out from heat and put away.
4. Warm up a grill pan in a med-high temp.
5. Thread the marinated tofu cubes onto the soaked bamboo skewers.
6. Grill the tofu skewers for 3-4 minutes on all sides, or 'til mildly charred and heated through.
7. Present the tofu satay skewers with the peanut sauce on the side for dipping.

Per serving: Calories: 320kcal; Fat: 18g; Carbs: 25g; Protein: 22g; Sugar: 12g; Sodium: 620mg; Potassium: 620mg; Glycemic index: 15

18. Fruit Salsa with Cinnamon Pita Chips

Recipe type:

Difficulty: Easy · **Preparation time:** 15 minutes
Cooking time: 10 minutes · **Servings:** 2
Ingredients:

For the fruit salsa:

- 1 apple, diced
- 1 pear, diced
- 1 cup strawberries, diced
- 1 tbsp. lemon juice
- 1 tbsp. honey or maple syrup
- 1 tsp. chopped fresh mint (optional)

For the cinnamon pita chips:

- 2 whole wheat pita breads
- 1 tbsp. olive oil
- 1 tsp. ground cinnamon
- 1 tbsp. honey or maple syrup (optional)

Directions:

1. Warm up the oven to 375 deg.F.
2. In your mixing bowl, blend the diced apple, pear, strawberries, lemon juice, honey or maple syrup, and chopped fresh mint (if using). Stir 'til well blended.

3. Cover the fruit salsa then put in the fridge 'til ready to serve.
4. Cut each whole wheat pita bread into 8 wedges.
5. In your small bowl, whisk collectively the olive oil and ground cinnamon.
6. Brush both sides of each pita wedge using the cinnamon oil mixture.
7. Place pita wedges in a one layer on your baking sheet.
8. Bake in to your warmed up oven for 8-10 minutes, or 'til crisp and golden brown.
9. If desired, drizzle the baked pita chips with additional honey or maple syrup.
10. Present the fruit salsa with the cinnamon pita chips.

Per serving: Calories: 250kcal; Fat: 7g; Carbs: 47g; Protein: 4g; Sugar: 24g; Sodium: 200mg; Potassium: 320mg; Glycemic index: 40

19. Beetroot and Feta Bruschetta

Recipe type:

Difficulty: Medium · **Preparation time:** 15 minutes
Cooking time: 5 minutes · **Servings:** 2
Ingredients:

- 4 slices of whole grain bread
- 1 medium beetroot, cooked and diced
- 2 oz feta cheese, crumbled
- 2 tbsps. balsamic glaze
- 1 tbsp. chopped fresh parsley
- 1 tbsp. olive oil
- Salt and pepper as required

Directions:
1. Warm up the oven to 375 deg.F. Put the bread slices on your baking sheet and brush them using olive oil.
2. Bake in to your warmed up oven for 5 minutes, or 'til mildly toasted.
3. In your mixing bowl, blend the diced beetroot, crumbled feta cheese, chopped fresh parsley, balsamic glaze, salt, and pepper. Stir 'til well blended.
4. Take out the toasted bread slices from the oven then let them cool mildly.
5. Top each slice of toasted bread with the beetroot and feta mixture.
6. Present instantly.

Per serving: Calories: 250kcal; Fat: 9g; Carbs: 32g; Protein: 11g; Sugar: 12g; Sodium: 480mg; Potassium: 330mg; Glycemic index: 55

20. Greek Yogurt Dip with Fresh Veggies

Recipe type:

Difficulty: Easy · **Preparation time:** 10 minutes
Cooking time: 0 minutes · **Servings:** 2
Ingredients:

- 1/2 cup Greek yogurt
- 1 tbsp. lemon juice
- 1 clove garlic, crushed
- 1 tbsp. chopped fresh dill
- Salt and pepper as required
- Assorted fresh vegetables for dipping (e.g., carrots, cucumber, bell peppers, cherry tomatoes)

Directions:
1. In your mixing bowl, blend the lemon juice, crushed garlic, Greek yogurt, and chopped fresh dill.
2. Flavour using salt and pepper as required, and mix 'til well blended.
3. Put the yogurt dip to a serving bowl.
4. Organize the assorted fresh vegetables around the dip on your serving platter.
5. Present instantly.

Per serving: Calories: 60kcal; Fat: 0g; Carbs: 6g; Protein: 8g; Sugar: 4g; Sodium: 50mg; Potassium: 250mg; Glycemic index: 15

21. Grilled Zucchini Rolls with Herbed Goat Cheese

Recipe type:
Difficulty: Medium
Preparation time: 20 minutes
Cooking time: 10 minutes
Servings: 2 (8 rolls)
Ingredients:

- 2 small zucchini, finely cut lengthwise
- 4 oz herbed goat cheese
- 2 tbsps. chopped fresh basil
- 2 tbsps. chopped fresh parsley
- 1 tbsp. chopped fresh chives
- 1 tbsp. olive oil
- Salt and pepper as required

Directions:

1. Warm up a grill pan in a med-high temp.
2. In your small bowl, blend collectively the herbed goat cheese, chopped fresh basil, chopped fresh parsley, and chopped fresh chives.
3. Put a thin layer of the goat cheese mixture onto each zucchini slice.
4. Roll up each zucchini slice and secure with a toothpick if necessary.
5. Brush the zucchini rolls using olive oil and flavour using salt and pepper.
6. Grill the zucchini rolls for 2-3 minutes on all sides, or 'til grill marks appear and the zucchini is tender.
7. Take out from the grill then let them cool mildly prior to presenting.
8. Present warm or at room temp.

Per serving: Calories: 180kcal; Fat: 14g; Carbs: 6g; Protein: 8g; Sugar: 3g; Sodium: 180mg; Potassium: 520mg; Glycemic index: 15

Snacks Recipes

22. Homemade Granola Bars with Oats, Nuts, and Dried Fruit

Recipe type:

Difficulty: Medium · **Preparation time:** 15 minutes
Cooking time: 20 minutes · **Servings:** 8 bars

Ingredients:

- 1 1/2 cups rolled oats
- 1/2 cup chopped nuts (e.g., almonds, walnuts, or pecans)
- 1/4 cup dried fruit (e.g., raisins, cranberries, or apricots), chopped
- 1/4 cup honey or maple syrup
- 1/4 cup almond butter or a peanut butter
- 1 tbsp. coconut oil
- 1/2 tsp. vanilla extract
- Pinch of salt

Directions:

1. Warm up the oven to 350 deg.F. Line a baking dish using parchment paper.
2. In your big bowl, blend rolled oats, chopped nuts, and dried fruit.
3. In your small saucepan, heat honey (or maple syrup), coconut oil, almond butter (or peanut butter), vanilla extract, then a pinch of salt over low heat. Stir 'til smooth and well blended.
4. Put the wet mixture over the dry components in the bowl. Mix 'til everything is uniformly covered.
5. After placing the mixture in the baking dish that has been prepared, push it down strongly to ensure that it adheres uniformly.
6. Bake in to your warmed up oven for 18-20 minutes, or 'til the edges are golden brown.
7. Take out from the oven then let it cool entirely in the baking dish.
8. Once cooled, cut into bars then store in your sealed container.

Per serving: Calories: 200kcal; Fat: 10g; Carbs: 25g; Protein: 5g; Sugar: 10g; Sodium: 20mg; Potassium: 180mg; Glycemic index: 45

23. Chia Seed Pudding with Fresh Fruit Topping

Recipe type:

Difficulty: Medium · **Preparation time:** 10 minutes
Cooking time: 0 minutes · **Servings:** 2

Ingredients:

- 1/4 cup chia seeds
- 1 cup unsweetened almond milk
- 1 tbsp. maple syrup (optional)
- 1/2 tsp. vanilla extract
- Fresh fruit for topping (e.g., berries, cut bananas, or mango chunks)

Directions:

1. In your mixing bowl, whisk collectively chia seeds, almond milk, maple syrup (if using), and vanilla extract 'til well blended.
2. Cover your bowl then put in the fridge for almost 2 hours or overnight, 'til the mixture thickens and becomes pudding-like.
3. Stir the chia seed pudding prior to presenting to break up any clumps.
4. Split pudding into serving bowls and top with fresh fruit.
5. Present chilled.

Per serving: Calories: 150kcal; Fat: 8g; Carbs: 16g; Protein: 5g; Sugar: 7g; Sodium: 80mg; Potassium: 180mg; Glycemic index: 15

24. Vegan Sushi Rolls with Avocado and Cucumber

Recipe type:
Difficulty: Hard
Preparation time: 30 minutes
Cooking time: 0 minutes
Servings: 2
Ingredients:

- 2 nori seaweed sheets
- 1 cup cooked sushi rice
- 1/2 avocado, cut
- 1/2 cucumber, julienned
- Soy sauce and wasabi for presenting (optional)
- Pickled ginger for presenting (optional)

Directions:

1. Put a nori seaweed sheet shiny side down on a bamboo sushi mat or your clean kitchen towel.
2. Put a thin layer of cooked sushi rice over your nori sheet, leaving a 1" border along the top edge.
3. Organize avocado slices and cucumber julienne in a line across the center of the rice.
4. Using the bamboo mat or towel, roll up the sushi firmly, starting from bottom edge and rolling towards the top edge.
5. Wet the top edge of your nori sheet using a small amout of water to seal the roll.
6. Repeat using the rest of the nori sheet and components.
7. Use your sharp knife to slice each sushi roll into 6-8 pieces.
8. Present the vegan sushi rolls with soy sauce, wasabi, and pickled ginger if wanted.

Per serving: Calories: 200kcal; Fat: 9g; Carbs: 28g; Protein: 4g; Sugar: 1g; Sodium: 10mg; Potassium: 320mg; Glycemic index: 30

25. Seaweed Salad with Sesame Dressing

Recipe type:
Difficulty: Hard
Preparation time: 15 minutes
Cooking time: 0 minutes
Servings: 2
Ingredients:

- 2 cups mixed seaweed salad (e.g., wakame, hijiki, or kombu)
- 2 tbsps. rice vinegar
- 1 tbsp. soy sauce
- 1 tbsp. sesame oil
- 1 tsp. honey or maple syrup
- 1 tsp. grated ginger
- 1 tsp. sesame seeds
- 1 green onion, finely cut (optional)
- 1/2 tsp. chili flakes (optional)

Directions:

1. Rinse the seaweed salad under cold water and drain well.
2. In your small bowl, whisk collectively honey (or maple syrup), rice vinegar, soy sauce, sesame oil, grated ginger, sesame seeds, cut green onion, and chili flakes (if using).
3. Put the sesame dressing over the seaweed salad then toss 'til uniformly covered.
4. Present instantly.

Per serving: Calories: 120kcal; Fat: 7g; Carbs: 10g; Protein: 5g; Sugar: 2g; Sodium: 600mg; Potassium: 150mg; Glycemic index: 30

26. Trail Mix with Nuts, Seeds, and Dried Fruit

Recipe type:

Difficulty: Easy · **Preparation time:** 5 minutes
Cooking time: 0 minutes · **Servings:** 2

Ingredients:

- 1/4 cup almonds
- 1/4 cup cashews
- 2 tbsps. pumpkin seeds
- 2 tbsps. sunflower seeds
- 2 tbsps. dried cranberries
- 2 tbsps. raisins

Directions:

1. In your bowl, blend almonds, cashews, pumpkin seeds, sunflower seeds, dried cranberries, and raisins.
2. Blend thoroughly 'til uniformly distributed.
3. Present the trail mix as a nutritious snack.

Per serving: Calories: 240kcal; Fat: 15g; Carbs: 22g; Protein: 7g; Sugar: 10g; Sodium: 5mg; Potassium: 310mg; Glycemic index: 30

27. Carrot Sticks with Hummus

Recipe type:

Difficulty: Easy · **Preparation time:** 10 minutes
Cooking time: 0 minutes · **Servings:** 2

Ingredients:

- 2 carrots, skinned and cut into sticks
- 1/4 cup hummus

Directions:

1. Peel the carrots and cut them into sticks.
2. Present the carrot sticks with hummus for dipping.
3. Relish as a nutritious snack.

Per serving: Calories: 90kcal; Fat: 4g; Carbs: 12g; Protein: 3g; Sugar: 4g; Sodium: 150mg; Potassium: 340mg; Glycemic index: 35

28. Quinoa Salad Jars with Veggies and Lemon Herb Dressing

Recipe type:

Difficulty: Medium · **Preparation time:** 20 minutes
Cooking time: 15 minutes (quinoa) · **Servings:** 2

Ingredients:

- 1 cup cooked quinoa
- 1 cup mixed vegetables (e.g., cucumber, bell peppers, cherry tomatoes, carrots)
- 2 tbsps. lemon herb dressing

For the lemon herb dressing:

- 2 tbsps. olive oil
- 1 tbsp. lemon juice
- 1 tbsp. chopped fresh herbs (e.g., parsley, basil, or cilantro)
- Salt and pepper as required

Directions:

1. In your small bowl, whisk collectively olive oil, lemon juice, chopped fresh herbs, salt, and pepper to create the dressing.
2. Split the cooked quinoa uniformly between two jars.
3. Layer the mixed vegetables on top of the quinoa in each jar.
4. Drizzle the lemon herb dressing over the vegetables.
5. Seal jars then store them in the fridge 'til ready to eat.
6. When ready to eat, shake the jars to distribute the dressing and relish the quinoa salad.

Per serving: Calories: 300kcal; Fat: 14g; Carbs: 36g; Protein: 8g; Sugar: 4g; Sodium: 20mg; Potassium: 420mg; Glycemic index: 35

29. Apple Slices with Almond Butter

Recipe type:
Difficulty: Easy
Preparation time: 5 minutes
Cooking time: 0 minutes
Servings: 2
Ingredients:

- 1 apple, cored then cut
- 2 tbsps. almond butter

Directions:

1. Wash and core the apple, then slice it into thin wedges.
2. Present the apple slices with almond butter for dipping.
3. Relish instantly.

Per serving: Calories: 150kcal; Fat: 8g; Carbs: 18g; Protein: 3g; Sugar: 11g; Sodium: 10mg; Potassium: 190mg; Glycemic index: 30

30. Cottage Cheese with Pineapple Chunks

Recipe type:
Difficulty: Easy
Preparation time: 5 minutes
Cooking time: 0 minutes
Servings: 2
Ingredients:

- 1 cup cottage cheese
- 1/2 cup pineapple chunks (fresh or canned in juice)

Directions:

1. Spoon the cottage cheese into serving bowls.
2. Top with pineapple chunks.
3. Present instantly.

Per serving: Calories: 150kcal; Fat: 2g; Carbs: 18g; Protein: 15g; Sugar: 15g; Sodium: 400mg; Potassium: 220mg; Glycemic index: 45

31. Banana Chips

Recipe type:
Difficulty: Easy
Preparation time: 5 minutes
Cooking time: 2 hours
Servings: 2
Ingredients:

- 2 ripe bananas

Directions:

1. Warm up the oven to 200 deg.F. Cover a baking sheet with parchment paper and put it away.
2. Peel the bananas then slice them into thin rounds.
3. Put the banana slices on your organized baking sheet in a one layer.
4. Bake in to your warmed up oven for 2 hours, turning them over on the halfway point, or 'til the banana chips are crisp and golden brown.
5. Take out from the oven then let them cool entirely prior to presenting.
6. Store any leftovers in your sealed container for future snacking.

Per serving: Calories: 90kcal; Fat: 0g; Carbs: 23g; Protein: 1g; Sugar: 12g; Sodium: 0mg; Potassium: 320mg; Glycemic index: 50

First Courses of Land

32. Whole Wheat Pasta Primavera with Roasted Vegetables

Recipe type:
Difficulty: Hard
Preparation time: 20 minutes
Cooking time: 30 minutes
Servings: 2
Ingredients:

- 6 oz whole wheat pasta
- 2 cups mixed vegetables (e.g., bell peppers, zucchini, cherry tomatoes, broccoli)
- 2 tbsps. olive oil
- 2 pieces garlic, crushed
- 1/4 tsp. red pepper flakes
- Salt and pepper as required
- 1/4 cup grated Parmesan cheese (optional)
- Fresh basil leaves for garnish (optional)

Directions:

1. Warm up the oven to 400 deg.F.
2. Cook the whole wheat pasta using the package guidelines 'til al dente. Drain and put away.
3. Meanwhile, prepare the mixed vegetables. Cut them into bite-sized pieces if needed.
4. Disperse the mixed vegetables on your baking sheet, drizzle using olive oil, crushed garlic, red pepper flakes, salt, and pepper. Toss to coat uniformly.
5. Roast the vegetables in to your warmed up oven for 20-25 minutes, or 'til tender and mildly browned.
6. In your big skillet, heat a tbsp. of olive oil in a middling temp. Put the cooked pasta and roasted vegetables to your skillet. Toss to blend and heat through.
7. Present the whole wheat pasta primavera hot, garnished using grated Parmesan cheese and fresh basil leaves if wanted.

Per serving: Calories: 400kcal; Fat: 14g; Carbs: 60g; Protein: 12g; Sugar: 5g; Sodium: 250mg; Potassium: 450mg; Glycemic index: 45

33. Spinach Salad with Strawberries and Almonds

Recipe type:
Difficulty: Easy
Preparation time: 10 minutes
Cooking time: 0 minutes
Servings: 2
Ingredients:

- 4 cups baby spinach leaves
- 1/2 cup fresh strawberries, cut
- 1/4 cup almonds, cut
- 2 tbsps. balsamic vinegar
- 1 tbsp. extra virgin olive oil
- Salt and pepper as required

Directions:

1. In your big bowl, blend baby spinach leaves, cut strawberries, then cut almonds.
2. In your small bowl, whisk collectively salt, balsamic vinegar, extra virgin olive oil, and pepper to create the dressing.
3. Put the dressing over the salad then toss 'til uniformly covered.
4. Split the spinach salad between two plates and serve instantly.

Per serving: Calories: 180kcal; Fat: 13g; Carbs: 13g; Protein: 6g; Sugar: 5g; Sodium: 20mg; Potassium: 460mg; Glycemic index: 20

34. Vegetable and Bean Chili

Recipe type:
Difficulty: Medium
Preparation time: 15 minutes
Cooking time: 30 minutes
Servings: 2
Ingredients:

- 1 tbsp. olive oil
- 1 onion, diced
- 2 pieces garlic, crushed
- 1 bell pepper, diced
- 1 zucchini, diced
- 1 carrot, diced
- 1 can (15 oz) diced tomatoes
- 1 can (15 oz) kidney beans
- 1 cup vegetable broth
- 1 tbsp. chili powder
- 1 tsp. ground cumin
- Salt and pepper as required
- Fresh cilantro for garnish (optional)
- Avocado slices for presenting (optional)
- Tortilla chips for presenting (optional)

Directions:

1. In your big pot, warm olive oil in a middling temp. Include diced onion and garlic, sauté 'til softened, around 3-4 minutes.
2. Include diced bell pepper, zucchini, and carrot to the pot. Cook for extra 5 minutes, mixing irregularly.
3. Stir in diced tomatoes, kidney beans, vegetable broth, chili powder, ground cumin, salt, and pepper. Bring to a simmer.
4. Decrease the temp., cover, then let the chili simmer for 20-25 minutes, mixing irregularly, 'til vegetables are tender and flavors are well blended.
5. Adjust seasoning using salt and pepper if needed.
6. Present hot, garnished using fresh cilantro if wanted. Present with avocado slices and tortilla chips if wanted.

Per serving: Calories: 350kcal; Fat: 8g; Carbs: 60g; Protein: 15g; Sugar: 15g; Sodium: 900mg; Potassium: 1100mg; Glycemic index: 30

35. Lentil Soup with Vegetables

Recipe type:
Difficulty: Easy
Preparation time: 10 minutes
Cooking time: 30 minutes
Servings: 2
Ingredients:

- 1/2 cup dried lentils
- 3 cups vegetable broth
- 1 carrot, diced
- 1 celery stalk, diced
- 1/2 onion, diced
- 1 garlic clove, crushed
- 1/2 tsp. dried thyme
- Salt and pepper as required
- Fresh parsley for garnish (optional)

Directions:

1. In your big pot, blend dried lentils, vegetable broth, carrot, celery, onion, garlic, and dried thyme.
2. Boil the mixture, then decrease the temp. then let it simmer for 25-30 minutes, or 'til the lentils and vegetables are tender.
3. Flavour using salt and pepper as required.
4. Ladle lentil soup into bowls then garnish with fresh parsley if wanted.
5. Present hot.

Per serving: Calories: 200kcal; Fat: 1g; Carbs: 35g; Protein: 13g; Sugar: 5g; Sodium: 690mg; Potassium: 700mg; Glycemic index: 25

36. Minestrone Soup with Whole Wheat Pasta

Recipe type:
Difficulty: Easy
Preparation time: 10 minutes
Cooking time: 30 minutes
Servings: 2
Ingredients:

- 4 cups vegetable broth
- 1/2 cup whole wheat pasta (e.g., penne or fusilli)
- 1 carrot, diced
- 1 celery stalk, diced
- 1/2 onion, diced
- 1 garlic clove, crushed
- 1/2 cup canned diced tomatoes
- 1/2 cup kidney beans
- 1/2 tsp. dried oregano
- Salt and pepper as required
- Fresh parsley for garnish (optional)

Directions:

1. In your big pot, bring vegetable broth to a boil.
2. Include whole wheat pasta, diced carrot, diced celery, diced onion, crushed garlic, canned diced tomatoes, kidney beans, and dried oregano to the pot.
3. Decrease the temp. then let the soup simmer for 20-25 minutes, or 'til the pasta and vegetables are tender.
4. Flavour using salt and pepper as required.
5. Ladle the minestrone soup into bowls then garnish with fresh parsley if wanted.
6. Present hot.

Per serving: Calories: 250kcal; Fat: 1g; Carbs: 48g; Protein: 12g; Sugar: 7g; Sodium: 970mg; Potassium: 570mg; Glycemic index: 40

37. Spaghetti Squash with Marinara Sauce

Recipe type:
Difficulty: Medium
Preparation time: 10 minutes
Cooking time: 40 minutes
Servings: 2
Ingredients:

- 1 spaghetti squash, divided and seeds taken out
- 1 tbsp. olive oil
- Salt and pepper as required
- 2 cups marinara sauce (store-bought or homemade)
- Fresh basil leaves for garnish (optional)
- Vegan Parmesan cheese for presenting (optional)

Directions:

1. Warm up the oven to 400 deg.F. Place spaghetti squash halves cut-side up on your baking sheet.
2. Drizzle olive oil over the spaghetti squash halves and flavour using salt and pepper.
3. Roast in to your warmed up oven for 30-40 minutes, or 'til the flesh is tender and simply pierced using a fork.
4. Take out from the oven then let the spaghetti squash cool mildly.
5. Using your fork, create strands of spaghetti squash by scraping the flesh of the squash.
6. Split the spaghetti squash strands between two plates and top with marinara sauce.
7. Garnish using fresh basil leaves and vegan Parmesan cheese if wanted.
8. Present hot.

Per serving: Calories: 200kcal; Fat: 7g; Carbs: 35g; Protein: 5g; Sugar: 10g; Sodium: 700mg; Potassium: 600mg; Glycemic index: 40

38. Cauliflower Fried Rice with Tofu

Recipe type:
Difficulty: Hard
Preparation time: 20 minutes
Cooking time: 20 minutes
Servings: 2
Ingredients:

- 1 small head cauliflower, grated
- 6 oz extra firm tofu, pressed and cubed
- 2 tbsps. sesame oil
- 2 pieces garlic, crushed
- 1 tbsp. ginger, crushed
- 1 cup mixed vegetables (e.g., peas, carrots, corn)
- 2 tbsps. low-sodium soy sauce
- 1 tbsp. rice vinegar
- 1 tsp. sesame seeds for garnish (optional)
- Sliced green onions for garnish (optional)

Directions:

1. Press your tofu to take out extra water then cut it into small cubes.
2. Heat one tbsp. of your sesame oil in a huge skillet or wok in a middling temp. Put the tofu cubes then cook 'til golden brown on all sides. Take out from the skillet and put away.
3. In the same skillet, place the rest of the tbsp. of sesame oil. Include crushed garlic and ginger, sauté for 1-2 minutes 'til fragrant.
4. Put the mixed vegetables to your skillet then cook 'til tender, around 5-7 minutes.
5. Stir in the grated cauliflower then cooked tofu cubes. Cook for extra 5 minutes, mixing irregularly.
6. Include low-sodium soy sauce and rice vinegar to your skillet. Stir to blend then cook 2-3 minutes more.
7. Garnish using sesame seeds then cut green onions if wanted.
8. Present hot.

Per serving: Calories: 300kcal; Fat: 18g; Carbs: 20g; Protein: 20g; Sugar: 5g; Sodium: 450mg; Potassium: 900mg; Glycemic index: 20

39. Tomato Basil Bruschetta

Recipe type:
Difficulty: Easy
Preparation time: 10 minutes
Cooking time: 0 minutes
Servings: 2
Ingredients:

- 4 slices whole grain bread
- 2 ripe tomatoes, diced
- 2 pieces garlic, crushed
- 1/4 cup fresh basil leaves, chopped
- 2 tbsps. extra virgin olive oil
- Salt and pepper as required

Directions:

1. Warm up the oven to 400 deg.F. Put the whole grain bread slices on your baking sheet then toast them in your oven for 5-7 minutes, or 'til mildly golden.
2. In your bowl, blend diced tomatoes, crushed garlic, chopped basil, extra virgin olive oil, salt, and pepper.
3. Spoon your tomato mixture onto the toasted bread slices.
4. Present the tomato basil bruschetta instantly.

Per serving: Calories: 180kcal; Fat: 9g; Carbs: 20g; Protein: 5g; Sugar: 5g; Sodium: 300mg; Potassium: 320mg; Glycemic index: 30

40. Stuffed Portobello Mushrooms with Quinoa and Spinach

Recipe type:
Difficulty: Hard
Preparation time: 20 minutes
Cooking time: 25 minutes
Servings: 2
Ingredients:

- 2 big Portobello mushrooms, stems taken out
- 1/2 cup quinoa, washed
- 1 cup vegetable broth
- 1 tbsp. olive oil
- 1/2 onion, diced
- 2 pieces garlic, crushed
- 2 cups baby spinach
- 1/4 cup grated Parmesan cheese (optional)
- Salt and pepper as required
- Fresh parsley for garnish (optional)

Directions:

1. Warm up the oven to 375 deg.F. Put the Portobello mushrooms on your baking sheet lined using parchment paper, gill side up.
2. In your saucepan, bring vegetable broth to a boil. Include quinoa, decrease temp. to low, cover, then simmer for 15 minutes or 'til quinoa is cooked and liquid is immersed. Take out from heat then let it cool.
3. In your skillet, warm olive oil in a middling temp. Include diced onion and crushed garlic, sauté 'til softened, around 3-4 minutes.
4. Include baby spinach to your skillet then cook 'til wilted, about 2-3 minutes.
5. Stir in cooked quinoa and grated Parmesan cheese if using. Flavour using salt and pepper as required.
6. Spoon the quinoa and spinach mixture into the Portobello mushrooms, dividing uniformly.
7. Bake in to your warmed up oven for 20-25 minutes, or 'til the mushrooms are tender.
8. Garnish using fresh parsley if wanted.
9. Present hot.

Per serving: Calories: 250kcal; Fat: 8g; Carbs: 35g; Protein: 10g; Sugar: 5g; Sodium: 500mg; Potassium: 800mg; Glycemic index: 20

Seafood First Courses

41. Stuffed Squid with Quinoa and Spinach

Recipe type:
Difficulty: Hard
Preparation time: 30 minutes
Cooking time: 30 minutes
Servings: 2
Ingredients:

- 4 small squid tubes
- 1/2 cup cooked quinoa
- 1 cup fresh spinach, chopped
- 1/4 cup cherry tomatoes, diced
- 2 pieces garlic, crushed
- 1/4 cup feta cheese, crumbled
- 1 tbsp. olive oil
- Salt and pepper as required
- Lemon wedges for presenting

Directions:

1. Warm up the oven to 375 deg.F.
2. In your bowl, blend cooked quinoa, chopped fresh spinach, diced cherry tomatoes, crushed garlic, crumbled feta cheese, olive oil, salt, and pepper. Blend thoroughly.
3. Stuff each squid tube with the quinoa and spinach mixture, leaving some space at the top to secure with a toothpick.
4. Put the filled squid tubes in your baking dish and bake in to your warmed up oven for 25-30 minutes, 'til the squid is cooked through and tender.
5. Take out the toothpicks prior to presenting.
6. Present the filled squid hot, with lemon wedges on the side.

Per serving: Calories: 350kcal; Fat: 15g; Carbs: 25g; Protein: 25g; Sugar: 2g; Sodium: 600mg; Potassium: 800mg; Glycemic index: 20

42. Lemon Herb Baked Cod Fillets

Recipe type:
Difficulty: Easy
Preparation time: 10 minutes
Cooking time: 15 minutes
Servings: 2
Ingredients:

- 2 cod fillets (6 oz each)
- 2 tbsps. olive oil
- 2 tbsps. lemon juice
- 2 pieces garlic, crushed
- 1 tsp. chopped fresh thyme
- 1 tsp. chopped fresh rosemary
- Salt and pepper as required
- Lemon slices for garnish (optional)

Directions:

1. Warm up the oven to 400 deg.F.
2. In your small bowl, whisk collectively olive oil, lemon juice, crushed garlic, chopped fresh thyme, chopped fresh rosemary, salt, and pepper.
3. Put the cod fillets on your baking sheet lined using parchment paper.
4. Brush the lemon herb mixture over the cod fillets, coating them uniformly.
5. Bake in to your warmed up oven for 12-15 minutes, or 'til the cod is cooked through and flakes simply using a fork.
6. Present hot, garnished using lemon slices if wanted.

Per serving: Calories: 250kcal; Fat: 12g; Carbs: 2g; Protein: 30g; Sugar: 1g; Sodium: 300mg; Potassium: 600mg; Glycemic index: 10

43. Seafood Paella with Brown Rice

Recipe type:
Difficulty: Medium
Preparation time: 20 minutes
Cooking time: 40 minutes
Servings: 2
Ingredients:

- 1 cup brown rice
- 1 tbsp. olive oil
- 1 onion, diced
- 2 pieces garlic, crushed
- 1 red bell pepper, diced
- 1 yellow bell pepper, diced
- 1/2 cup frozen peas
- 8 oz mixed seafood (e.g., shrimp, mussels, squid)
- 1 tsp. smoked paprika
- 1/2 tsp. saffron threads
- 2 cups vegetable broth
- Salt and pepper as required
- Lemon wedges for presenting

Directions:

1. Cook the brown rice using the package guidelines. Put away.
2. In your big skillet or paella pan, warm olive oil in a middling temp. Include diced onion and crushed garlic. Cook 'til softened, around 3-4 minutes.
3. Include diced red bell pepper and yellow bell pepper to your skillet. Cook for extra 3-4 minutes.
4. Stir in frozen peas, mixed seafood, smoked paprika, and saffron threads. Cook for 2-3 minutes.
5. Include cooked brown rice to your skillet. Pour vegetable broth over the rice and seafood mixture.
6. Flavour using salt and pepper as required. Stir to blend.
7. Cover the skillet then simmer for 20-25 minutes, or 'til the liquid is immersed and the rice is tender.
8. Take out from heat then let it sit for a couple of minutes prior to presenting.
9. Present the seafood paella hot, with lemon wedges on the side.

Per serving: Calories: 450kcal; Fat: 10g; Carbs: 70g; Protein: 25g; Sugar: 5g; Sodium: 600mg; Potassium: 600mg; Glycemic index: 45

44. Salmon and Quinoa Salad with Lemon-Dill Dressing

Recipe type:
Difficulty: Easy
Preparation time: 20 minutes
Cooking time: 15 minutes
Servings: 2
Ingredients:

- 2 salmon fillets (6 oz each)
- 1 cup cooked quinoa
- 2 cups mixed salad greens
- 1 cucumber, cut
- 1/4 cup cherry tomatoes, divided
- 2 tbsps. chopped fresh dill
- 2 tbsps. olive oil
- Juice of 1 lemon
- Salt and pepper as required

Directions:

1. Warm up the oven to 375 deg.F. Place salmon fillets on your baking sheet lined using parchment paper. Flavour using salt and pepper.

2. Bake in to your warmed up oven for 12-15 minutes, or 'til salmon is cooked through and flakes simply using a fork.
3. In your big bowl, blend cooked quinoa, mixed salad greens, cut cucumber, cherry tomatoes, and chopped fresh dill.
4. In your small bowl, whisk collectively olive oil and lemon juice to create the dressing. Flavour using salt and pepper as required.
5. Put the dressing to the salad then toss 'til well blended.
6. Split the salad between two plates and top each with a baked salmon fillet.
7. Present instantly.

Per serving: Calories: 450kcal; Fat: 20g; Carbs: 35g; Protein: 35g; Sugar: 5g; Sodium: 300mg; Potassium: 1200mg; Glycemic index: 20

45. Seafood Risotto with Asparagus and Peas

Recipe type:
Difficulty: Hard
Preparation time: 10 minutes
Cooking time: 40 minutes
Servings: 2
Ingredients:

- 1 cup Arborio rice
- 4 cups seafood or vegetable broth
- 1 tbsp. olive oil
- 1 onion, finely chopped
- 2 pieces garlic, crushed
- 1/2 cup dry white wine
- 8 asparagus spears, cut into 1" pieces
- 1/2 cup fresh or frozen peas
- 8 oz mixed seafood (e.g., shrimp, scallops, mussels)
- 1/4 cup grated Parmesan cheese
- Salt and pepper as required
- Fresh parsley, chopped (for garnish)

Directions:
1. In your saucepan, heat the seafood or vegetable broth over low heat and keep it warm.
2. In your distinct big pot, warm olive oil in a middling temp. Include chopped onion and crushed garlic. Cook 'til softened, around 3-4 minutes.
3. Stir in Arborio rice then cook for extra 2 minutes, mixing regularly.
4. Pour in the dry white wine then cook 'til the wine has evaporated.
5. Include a ladleful of warm broth to the rice then stir 'til the liquid is immersed. Continue placing the broth, one ladleful at a time, mixing regularly, 'til the rice is creamy and tender, around 20-25 minutes.
6. Meanwhile, blanch the asparagus pieces and peas in boiling water for 2-3 minutes, then drain and put away.
7. In your distinct skillet, warm olive oil in a med-high temp. Put the mixed seafood then cook 'til just opaque, about 2-3 minutes.
8. Once the risotto is cooked, stir in the blanched asparagus, peas, cooked seafood, and grated Parmesan cheese. Flavour using salt and pepper as required.
9. Take out from heat then let it rest for a couple of minutes prior to presenting.
10. Garnish using chopped fresh parsley prior to presenting.
11. Present the seafood risotto hot.

Per serving: Calories: 500kcal; Fat: 10g; Carbs: 60g; Protein: 35g; Sugar: 5g; Sodium: 800mg; Potassium: 700mg; Glycemic index: 55

46. Seafood Salad with Greek Yogurt Dressing

Recipe type:
Difficulty: Easy
Preparation time: 15 minutes
Cooking time: 0 minutes
Servings: 2
Ingredients:

- 8 oz mixed seafood (e.g., cooked shrimp, crabmeat, and/or scallops)
- 2 cups mixed salad greens
- 1 cucumber, cut
- 1/2 cup cherry tomatoes, divided
- 1/4 cup cut red onion
- 2 tbsps. chopped fresh parsley
- 1/4 cup Greek yogurt
- 1 tbsp. lemon juice
- 1 tbsp. olive oil
- Salt and pepper as required

Directions:

1. In your big bowl, blend mixed seafood, mixed salad greens, cut cucumber, divided cherry tomatoes, cut red onion, and chopped fresh parsley.
2. In your small bowl, whisk collectively lemon juice, Greek yogurt, and olive oil to make dressing. Flavour using salt and pepper as required.
3. Put the Greek yogurt dressing over the seafood salad then toss 'til well blended.
4. Split the seafood salad between two plates.
5. Present instantly.

Per serving: Calories: 250kcal; Fat: 10g; Carbs: 15g; Protein: 25g; Sugar: 5g; Sodium: 400mg; Potassium: 600mg; Glycemic index: 20

47. Thai Coconut Curry Mussels

Recipe type:
Difficulty: Medium
Preparation time: 15 minutes
Cooking time: 10 minutes
Servings: 2
Ingredients:

- 2 lbs fresh mussels, cleaned and debearded
- 1 tbsp. coconut oil
- 1 onion, diced
- 2 pieces garlic, crushed
- 1 tbsp. red curry paste
- 1 can (14 oz) coconut milk
- 1 tbsp. fish sauce
- 1 tbsp. lime juice
- 1 tbsp. chopped fresh cilantro
- Salt and pepper as required

Directions:

1. In your big pot, heat coconut oil in a middling temp. Include diced onion and crushed garlic. Cook 'til softened, around 3-4 minutes.
2. Stir in red curry paste then cook for extra minute.
3. Include cleaned mussels to the pot. Pour in coconut milk, fish sauce, and lime juice.
4. Cover the pot then cook for 5-7 minutes, or 'til the mussels have opened.
5. Discard any unopened mussels.
6. Flavour using salt and pepper as required.
7. Garnish using chopped fresh cilantro prior to presenting.
8. Present the Thai coconut curry mussels hot.

Per serving: Calories: 400kcal; Fat: 20g; Carbs: 15g; Protein: 30g; Sugar: 5g; Sodium: 800mg; Potassium: 900mg; Glycemic index: 20

48. Cucumber and Smoked Salmon Roll-Ups

Recipe type:
Difficulty: Easy · **Preparation time:** 10 minutes
Cooking time: 0 minutes · **Servings:** 2
Ingredients:

- 4 oz smoked salmon slices
- 1 cucumber
- 1/4 cup cream cheese
- 2 tbsps. chopped fresh dill
- Lemon zest for garnish (optional)

Directions:

1. Using a vegetable peeler, slice your cucumber lengthwise into thin strips.
2. Lay out your smoked salmon slices and spread a thin layer of your cream cheese on each slice.
3. Put a cucumber strip on top of each smoked salmon slice.
4. Sprinkle chopped fresh dill over the cucumber strips.
5. Roll up the smoked salmon slices with the cucumber strips inside.
6. Organize the roll-ups on your serving plate.
7. Garnish using lemon zest if wanted.
8. Present instantly.

Per serving: Calories: 200kcal; Fat: 12g; Carbs: 5g; Protein: 15g; Sugar: 3g; Sodium: 500mg; Potassium: 600mg; Glycemic index: 10

49. Grilled Shrimp Skewers with Pineapple and Bell Pepper

Recipe type:
Difficulty: Medium · **Preparation time:** 20 minutes
Cooking time: 10 minutes · **Servings:** 2
Ingredients:

- 12 big shrimp, skinned and deveined
- 1 cup pineapple chunks
- 1 bell pepper, cut into chunks
- 1 tbsp. olive oil
- 1 tsp. smoked paprika
- 1/2 tsp. garlic powder
- Salt and pepper as required
- Wooden skewers, soaked in a water for 30 minutes

Directions:

1. Warm up the grill to med-high temp.
2. In your bowl, blend shrimp, pineapple chunks, bell pepper chunks, olive oil, smoked paprika, garlic powder, salt, and pepper. Toss to coat uniformly.
3. Thread the shrimp, pineapple, and bell pepper onto the wooden skewers.
4. Grill your skewers for 2-3 minutes on all sides, or 'til the shrimp are pink and opaque.
5. Take out the skewers from the grill and serve hot.

Per serving: Calories: 250kcal; Fat: 10g; Carbs: 20g; Protein: 20g; Sugar: 10g; Sodium: 300mg; Potassium: 450mg; Glycemic index: 40

50. Shrimp and Vegetable Stir-Fry with Brown Rice

Recipe type:
Difficulty: Easy · **Preparation time:** 15 minutes
Cooking time: 15 minutes · **Servings:** 2
Ingredients:

- 1 cup brown rice
- 8 oz big shrimp, skinned and deveined
- 2 cups mixed vegetables (e.g., bell peppers, broccoli, snap peas)
- 2 tbsps. soy sauce (low-sodium if available)
- 1 tbsp. sesame oil

- 2 pieces garlic, crushed
- 1 tsp. grated ginger
- Sesame seeds for garnish (optional)
- Sliced green onions for garnish (optional)

Directions:
1. Cook the brown rice using the package guidelines 'til tender. Drain and put away.
2. In your big skillet or wok, heat sesame oil in a med-high temp.
3. Place crushed garlic and grated ginger to your skillet. Stir-fry for 1 minute 'til fragrant.
4. Put the shrimp to your skillet then cook 'til pink and opaque, about 2-3 minutes on all sides. Take out from the skillet then put away.
5. In same skillet, include the mixed vegetables then stir-fry 'til tender-crisp, around 5-7 minutes.
6. Return the cooked shrimp to your skillet. Include soy sauce then cooked brown rice. Stir-fry for extra 2-3 minutes 'til everything is heated through and well blended.
7. Garnish using sesame seeds then cut green onions if wanted.
8. Present hot.

Per serving: Calories: 400kcal; Fat: 8g; Carbs: 60g; Protein: 25g; Sugar: 3g; Sodium: 600mg; Potassium: 800mg; Glycemic index: 30

51. Baked Cod with Roasted Vegetables

Recipe type:
Difficulty: Medium · **Preparation time:** 20 minutes
Cooking time: 20 minutes · **Servings:** 2
Ingredients:

- 2 cod fillets (6 oz each)
- 2 tbsps. olive oil
- 1 tsp. dried thyme
- 1 tsp. dried rosemary
- 1/2 tsp. garlic powder
- Salt and pepper as required
- 1 cup cherry tomatoes
- 1 zucchini, cut
- 1 yellow squash, cut
- 1 bell pepper, cut
- 1 red onion, cut

Directions:
1. Warm up the oven to 400 deg.F.
2. Place cod fillets on your baking sheet lined using parchment paper.
3. Drizzle olive oil over the cod fillets. Sprinkle dried thyme, dried rosemary, garlic powder, salt, and pepper on top.
4. In your distinct bowl, toss cherry tomatoes, cut zucchini, cut yellow squash, cut bell pepper, then cut red onion using olive oil, salt, and pepper.
5. Disperse the vegetable mixture around the cod fillets on the baking sheet.
6. Bake in to your warmed up oven for 20 minutes, or 'til the cod is cooked through and flakes simply using a fork.
7. Present the baked cod with roasted vegetables hot.

Per serving: Calories: 300kcal; Fat: 15g; Carbs: 20g; Protein: 25g; Sugar: 10g; Sodium: 300mg; Potassium: 800mg; Glycemic index: 35

Second Courses of Land

52. Turkey Chili with Beans and Corn

Recipe type:
Difficulty: Easy
Preparation time: 15 minutes
Cooking time: 30 minutes
Servings: 2
Ingredients:

- 1/2 lb. ground turkey
- 1 small onion, diced
- 2 pieces garlic, crushed
- 1 bell pepper, diced
- 1 can (14.5 oz) diced tomatoes
- 1 can (15 oz) kidney beans
- 1 cup corn kernels (fresh or frozen)
- 1 tbsp. chili powder
- 1 tsp. ground cumin
- Salt and pepper as required
- Olive oil for cooking

Directions:

1. Warm olive oil in a huge pot in a middling temp. Include diced onion and crushed garlic, then cook 'til onion becomes translucent, around 3-4 minutes.
2. Place ground turkey to the pot, breaking it apart with a spoon, then cook 'til it is no longer pink.
3. Stir in diced bell pepper, diced tomatoes, kidney beans, corn kernels, chili powder, ground cumin, salt, and pepper.
4. Simmer the chili, then decrease the temp. to low. Let it simmer for 20-25 minutes, mixing seldom, 'til flavors are well blended and the chili has thickened.
5. Adjust seasoning using more salt and pepper if needed.
6. Present the turkey chili hot with your favorite toppings such as green onions, cheese, or sour cream. Relish!

Per serving: Calories: 431kcal; Fat: 11g; Carbs: 53g; Protein: 37g; Sugar: 12g; Sodium: 786mg; Potassium: 1550mg; Glycemic index: 20

53. Lemon Garlic Chicken Skewers

Recipe type:
Difficulty: Easy
Preparation time: 15 minutes
Cooking time: 10 minutes
Servings: 2
Ingredients:

- 2 boneless, skinless chicken breasts, cubes
- 2 tbsps. olive oil
- 2 pieces garlic, crushed
- 1 lemon, juiced and zested
- 1 tsp. dried oregano
- Salt and pepper as required
- Wooden skewers, soaked in a water for 30 minutes

Directions:

1. In your bowl, blend olive oil, crushed garlic, lemon juice, lemon zest, dried oregano, salt, and pepper to make the marinade.
2. Put the chicken cubes to the marinade then toss to coat uniformly. Marinate in the fridge for almost 30 minutes.
3. Warm up grill or grill pan in a med-high temp.
4. Thread marinated chicken cubes onto the soaked wooden skewers.
5. Grill your chicken skewers for around 4-5 minutes on all sides, or 'til they are cooked through and have nice grill marks.
6. Present the lemon garlic chicken skewers hot with your choice of side dishes. Relish!

Per serving: Calories: 252kcal; Fat: 11g; Carbs: 3g; Protein: 34g; Sugar: 1g; Sodium: 70mg; Potassium: 417mg; Glycemic index: 1

54. Grilled Steak Salad with Balsamic Vinaigrette

Recipe type:
Difficulty: Medium
Preparation time: 15 minutes
Cooking time: 10 minutes (for steak)
Servings: 2
Ingredients:

- 1/2 lb. lean steak (e.g., sirloin or flank), about 1" dense
- Salt and pepper as required
- 4 cups mixed salad greens
- 1 cup cherry tomatoes, divided
- 1/2 cucumber, cut
- 1/4 red onion, finely cut
- 1/4 cup crumbled feta cheese
- 2 tbsps. balsamic vinegar
- 1 tbsp. olive oil
- 1 tsp. Dijon mustard
- 1 tsp. honey
- 1 clove garlic, crushed

Directions:

1. Warm up grill to med-high temp. Flavour steak using salt and pepper on both sides.
2. Grill steak for around 4-5 minutes on all sides for medium-rare, or 'til desired doneness is reached. Take out from grill then let it rest for a couple of minutes prior to cutting.
3. In your big bowl, blend mixed salad greens, cherry tomatoes, cucumber slices, red onion slices, and crumbled feta cheese.
4. In your small bowl, whisk collectively balsamic vinegar, olive oil, Dijon mustard, honey, and crushed garlic to create the dressing.
5. Slice grilled steak thinly against the grain.
6. Split the salad mixture between two plates. Organize cut steak on top.
7. Drizzle balsamic vinaigrette over the salad and steak.
8. Present the grilled steak salad instantly. Relish!

Per serving: Calories: 416kcal; Fat: 23g; Carbs: 16g; Protein: 37g; Sugar: 8g; Sodium: 402mg; Potassium: 1107mg; Glycemic index: 3

55. Chicken Piccata with Whole Wheat Pasta

Recipe type:
Difficulty: Medium
Preparation time: 15 minutes
Cooking time: 20 minutes
Servings: 2
Ingredients:

- 2 boneless, skinless chicken breasts, pounded
- Salt and pepper as required
- 1/4 cup all-purpose flour (gluten-free flour)
- 2 tbsps. olive oil
- 2 pieces garlic, crushed
- 1/2 cup chicken broth
- 1/4 cup fresh lemon juice
- 2 tbsps. capers, drained
- 2 tbsps. unsalted butter
- 2 tbsps. fresh parsley, chopped
- Cooked whole wheat pasta, for presenting

Directions:

1. Flavour both sides of the chicken breasts using salt and pepper. Dredge them in your flour, shaking off any extra.
2. Warm olive oil in a huge skillet in a med-high temp. Put the chicken breasts then cook 'til golden brown on both sides then cooked through, about 4-5 minutes on all

sides. Take out chicken from skillet and put away.
3. In the same skillet, include crushed garlic then cook for around 30 seconds 'til fragrant.
4. Pour chicken broth and lemon juice into your skillet, scraping up any caramelized bits from the bottom of pan. Bring the mixture to a simmer.
5. Stir in capers then cook for extra 2-3 minutes.
6. Decrease the temp. then include butter to your skillet, swirling 'til melted and the sauce is mildly thickened.
7. Return the chicken breasts to your skillet, spooning some sauce over them. Cook for extra 2-3 minutes to heat through.
8. Sprinkle chopped parsley over the chicken piccata.
9. Present the chicken piccata hot over cooked whole wheat pasta, spooning extra sauce over the top. Relish!

Per serving: Calories: 487kcal; Fat: 25g; Carbs: 32g; Protein: 35g; Sugar: 2g; Sodium: 724mg; Potassium: 582mg; Glycemic index: 45

56. Pan-Seared Duck Breast with Orange Glaze

Recipe type:
Difficulty: Hard
Preparation time: 10 minutes
Cooking time: 20 minutes
Servings: 2
Ingredients:

- 2 duck breast halves
- Salt and pepper as required
- 1 tbsp. olive oil
- 1/2 cup orange juice
- Zest of 1 orange
- 2 tbsps. honey
- 2 pieces garlic, crushed
- 1 tsp. fresh thyme leaves
- 1 tsp. cornstarch (optional, for thickening)

Directions:
1. Score the skin of your duck breasts in a crosshatch pattern, being careful not to penetrate into the meat. Flavour both sides of the duck breasts using salt and pepper.
2. Warm olive oil in your skillet in a med-high temp. Place duck breasts in the skillet, skin-side down, then cook for around 6-8 minutes 'til the skin is golden brown and crispy. Flip then cook for extra 3-4 minutes for medium-rare, or 'til desired doneness is reached. Take out duck breasts from skillet then let them rest on a cutting board.
3. In the same skillet, include crushed garlic then cook for around 30 seconds 'til fragrant. Include orange juice and grated orange peel, making sure to scrape off any caramelized residue stuck to the bottom of the pan.
4. Stir in honey and fresh thyme leaves. Let the sauce simmer then reduce by half, around 5-7 minutes. If desired, whisk in cornstarch slurry (1 tsp. cornstarch mixed + 1 tbsp. water) to thicken the sauce.
5. Slice duck breasts thinly against the grain and serve hot, drizzled with orange glaze. Relish!

Per serving: Calories: 415kcal; Fat: 24g; Carbs: 22g; Protein: 29g; Sugar: 18g; Sodium: 94mg; Potassium: 547mg; Glycemic index: 39

57. Pork Stir-Fry with Snow Peas and Water Chestnuts

Per serving: Calories: 406kcal; Fat: 15g; Carbs: 34g; Protein: 34g; Sugar: 15g; Sodium: 1173mg; Potassium: 944mg; Glycemic index: 65

Recipe type: 🚫 🍯
Difficulty: Medium
Preparation time: 15 minutes
Cooking time: 15 minutes
Servings: 2
Ingredients:

- 1/2 lb. pork tenderloin, finely cut
- 2 tbsps. soy sauce
- 1 tbsp. rice vinegar
- 1 tbsp. honey
- 1 tbsp. olive oil
- 2 pieces garlic, crushed
- 1/2 onion, finely cut
- 1 cup snow peas, trimmed
- 1 can (8 oz) water chestnuts, drained then cut
- Cooked rice, for presenting

Directions:

1. In your bowl, whisk collectively soy sauce, rice vinegar, and honey. Include cut pork tenderloin to the marinade then toss to coat. Let it marinate for almost 10 minutes.
2. Warm olive oil in a huge skillet or wok in a med-high temp. Include crushed garlic and finely cut onion, then stir-fry for around 1 minute.
3. Include marinated pork slices to your skillet then stir-fry for 3-4 minutes 'til browned then cooked through.
4. Include snow peas then cut water chestnuts to your skillet, and continue to stir-fry for extra 2-3 minutes 'til vegetables are tender-crisp.
5. Present the pork stir-fry hot over cooked rice. Relish!

Seafood Second Courses

58. Baked Tilapia with Tomato and Herb Relish

Recipe type:
Difficulty: Easy
Preparation time: 10 minutes
Cooking time: 15 minutes
Servings: 2
Ingredients:

- 2 tilapia fillets
- 2 tomatoes, diced
- 2 tbsps. fresh parsley, chopped
- 1 tbsp. fresh basil, chopped
- 1 tbsp. olive oil
- 2 pieces garlic, crushed
- Salt and pepper as required
- Lemon wedges for presenting

Directions:

1. Warm up oven to 400 deg.F. Cover a baking sheet with parchment paper and put it away.
2. Place tilapia fillets on your organized baking sheet.
3. In your bowl, blend olive oil, diced tomatoes, chopped parsley, chopped basil, crushed garlic, salt, and pepper to make the relish.
4. Spoon the tomato and herb relish over the tilapia fillets, dividing it uniformly between them.
5. Bake tilapia in to your warmed up oven for 12-15 minutes, or 'til fish flakes simply using a fork and is cooked through.
6. Present baked tilapia hot with lemon wedges on the side. Relish!

Per serving: Calories: 223kcal; Fat: 10g; Carbs: 6g; Protein: 28g; Sugar: 3g; Sodium: 78mg; Potassium: 835mg; Glycemic index: 15

59. Broiled Scallops with Garlic Butter

Recipe type:
Difficulty: Easy
Preparation time: 10 minutes
Cooking time: 10 minutes
Servings: 2
Ingredients:

- 8 big scallops
- 2 tbsps. unsalted butter, melted
- 2 pieces garlic, crushed
- 1 tbsp. lemon juice
- Salt and pepper as required
- Chopped fresh parsley for garnish (optional)
- Lemon wedges for presenting

Directions:

1. Warm up broiler on high heat.
2. Pat dry the scallops using paper towels and flavour them mildly using salt and pepper.
3. In your small bowl, blend collectively melted butter, crushed garlic, and lemon juice.
4. Place scallops on a broiler pan or baking sheet lined with aluminum foil.
5. Brush the garlic butter mixture over the scallops, coating them uniformly.
6. Broil scallops for 5 minutes on one side, then flip them over and broil for extra 3-4 minutes, or 'til they are opaque and mildly browned.
7. Garnish broiled scallops with chopped fresh parsley, if wanted, and serve hot with lemon wedges. Relish!

Per serving: Calories: 194kcal; Fat: 9g; Carbs: 4g; Protein: 23g; Sugar: 0g; Sodium: 395mg; Potassium: 388mg; Glycemic index: 0

60. Seafood Paella with Shrimp, Mussels, and Clams

Recipe type: 🚫 🌾
Difficulty: Medium
Preparation time: 20 minutes
Cooking time: 40 minutes
Servings: 2
Ingredients:

- 1 cup paella rice (Arborio or Bomba rice)
- 2 cups seafood or chicken broth
- 8 big shrimp, skinned and deveined
- 8 mussels, cleaned and debearded
- 8 small clams, scrubbed
- 2 tbsps. olive oil
- 1 onion, chopped
- 2 pieces garlic, crushed
- 1 red bell pepper, diced
- 1 tomato, diced
- 1 tsp. smoked paprika
- 1/2 tsp. saffron threads
- Salt and pepper as required
- Fresh parsley for garnish
- Lemon wedges for presenting

Directions:

1. In your small bowl, soak saffron threads in 2 tbsps. of warm water.
2. Warm olive oil in your paella pan or big skillet in a middling temp. Include chopped onion then cook 'til softened, around 5 minutes.
3. Place crushed garlic and diced red bell pepper to the pan, then cook for extra 2-3 minutes.
4. Stir in diced tomato, smoked paprika, and soaked saffron threads along with the water. Cook for 2-3 minutes 'til the tomato starts to break down.
5. Include paella rice to the pan then stir to coat the grains with the vegetable mixture.
6. Pour seafood or chicken broth into the pan and flavour using salt and pepper. Simmer then cook uncovered for around 15 minutes, mixing irregularly.
7. Organize skinned and deveined shrimp, cleaned mussels, and scrubbed clams on top of the rice mixture. Cover pan using a lid then cook for extra 10-15 minutes 'til the seafood is cooked through and the rice is tender.
8. Once done, garnish using fresh parsley and serve hot with lemon wedges on the side. Relish!

Per serving: Calories: 527kcal; Fat: 16g; Carbs: 62g; Protein: 34g; Sugar: 4g; Sodium: 1118mg; Potassium: 579mg; Glycemic index: 46

61. Grilled Lobster with Herb Butter

Recipe type:
Difficulty: Hard
Preparation time: 30 minutes
Cooking time: 10 minutes
Servings: 2
Ingredients:

- 2 whole lobsters, split in half lengthwise
- 4 tbsps. unsalted butter, melted
- 2 pieces garlic, crushed
- 1 tbsp. chopped fresh parsley
- 1 tbsp. chopped fresh thyme
- Salt and pepper as required
- Lemon wedges for presenting

Directions:

1. Warm up grill to med-high temp.
2. In your small bowl, blend melted unsalted butter, crushed garlic, chopped fresh parsley, chopped fresh thyme, salt, and pepper to make your herb butter.
3. Brush herb butter generously over the flesh side of each lobster half.
4. Place lobster halves, flesh side down, on the warmed up grill. Cook for 4-5 minutes 'til grill marks appear and the flesh is opaque.
5. Carefully flip lobster halves over and continue to grill for extra 4-5 minutes 'til the shells are bright red then the meat is cooked through.
6. Take out grilled lobster halves from the grill and transfer to serving plates.
7. Present hot with your lemon wedges on the side. Relish!

Per serving: Calories: 294kcal; Fat: 18g; Carbs: 2g; Protein: 32g; Sugar: 0g; Sodium: 553mg; Potassium: 440mg; Glycemic index: 1

62. Grilled Swordfish with Mango Salsa

Recipe type:
Difficulty: Easy · **Preparation time:** 15 minutes
Cooking time: 10 minutes · **Servings:** 2
Ingredients:

- 2 swordfish fillets
- 1 tbsp. olive oil
- Salt and pepper as required

For the mango salsa:

- 1 ripe mango, skinned and diced
- 1/4 cup diced red onion
- 1/4 cup diced red bell pepper
- 1 jalapeño, sowed and diced
- 2 tbsps. chopped fresh cilantro
- 1 tbsp. lime juice
- Salt as required

Directions:

1. Warm up grill to med-high temp.
2. Rub swordfish fillets using olive oil and flavour them using salt and pepper.
3. Grill swordfish fillets for 4-5 minutes on all sides, or 'til they are cooked through and have grill marks.
4. While swordfish is grilling, prepare the mango salsa. In your bowl, blend diced mango, diced red onion, diced red bell pepper, diced jalapeño, chopped fresh cilantro, lime juice, and salt. Blend thoroughly.
5. Once swordfish fillets are done, take them out from the grill and transfer to serving plates.
6. Top grilled swordfish with mango salsa and serve hot. Relish!

Per serving: Calories: 335kcal; Fat: 11g; Carbs: 18g; Protein: 40g; Sugar: 15g; Sodium: 107mg; Potassium: 933mg; Glycemic index: 40

63. Pan-Seared Sea Bass with Lemon Caper Sauce

Recipe type:
Difficulty: Medium
Preparation time: 15 minutes
Cooking time: 15 minutes
Servings: 2
Ingredients:

- 2 sea bass fillets
- Salt and pepper as required
- 2 tbsps. olive oil
- 2 tbsps. unsalted butter
- 2 pieces garlic, crushed
- Zest and juice of 1 lemon
- 2 tbsps. capers, drained
- Chopped fresh parsley for garnish

Directions:

1. Pat sea bass fillets dry with paper towels and flavour them generously using salt and pepper on both sides.
2. Warm olive oil in a huge skillet in a med-high temp. Include sea bass fillets to your skillet, skin-side down, then cook for around 5-6 minutes 'til the skin is crispy and golden brown.
3. Carefully flip sea bass fillets and include unsalted butter to your skillet. Continue to cook for extra 3-4 minutes 'til fish flakes simply using a fork and is cooked through.
4. Include crushed garlic, lemon zest, lemon juice, and capers to your skillet. Cook for extra 1-2 minutes 'til the sauce is heated through and fragrant.
5. Take out sea bass fillets from the skillet and transfer to serving plates. Spoon lemon caper sauce over the fillets.
6. Garnish using chopped fresh parsley and serve hot. Relish!

Per serving: Calories: 371kcal; Fat: 26g; Carbs: 7g; Protein: 28g; Sugar: 1g; Sodium: 648mg; Potassium: 564mg; Glycemic index: 5

64. Baked Cod with Lemon and Herbs

Recipe type:
Difficulty: Easy · **Preparation time:** 10 minutes
Cooking time: 15 minutes · **Servings:** 2
Ingredients:

- 2 cod fillets
- 1 lemon, cut
- 2 tbsps. olive oil
- 2 pieces garlic, crushed
- 1 tsp. dried thyme
- Salt and pepper as required

Directions:

1. Warm up oven to 400 deg.F. Cover a baking sheet with parchment paper and put it away.
2. Place cod fillets on your organized baking sheet.
3. Drizzle olive oil over the cod fillets. Sprinkle salt, crushed garlic, dried thyme, and pepper uniformly over the fillets.
4. Place lemon slices on top of each cod fillet.
5. Bake cod in to your warmed up oven for 12-15 minutes, or 'til fish flakes simply using a fork and is cooked through.
6. Present baked cod hot with your favorite side dishes. Relish!

Per serving: Calories: 268kcal; Fat: 15g; Carbs: 5g; Protein: 28g; Sugar: 1g; Sodium: 106mg; Potassium: 734mg; Glycemic index: 2

65. Coconut Curry Shrimp with Rice Noodles

Recipe type:
Difficulty: Medium
Preparation time: 15 minutes
Cooking time: 20 minutes
Servings: 2
Ingredients:

- 8 oz rice noodles
- 1 tbsp. coconut oil
- 1 onion, finely cut
- 2 pieces garlic, crushed
- 1 red bell pepper, finely cut
- 1 carrot, julienned
- 1 zucchini, julienned
- 1 tbsp. red curry paste
- 1 can (13.5 oz) coconut milk
- 1 tbsp. fish sauce
- 1 tbsp. brown sugar
- 12 big shrimp, skinned and deveined
- Juice of 1 lime
- Fresh cilantro for garnish

Directions:

1. Cook rice noodles using the package guidelines. Drain and put away.
2. In your big skillet, heat coconut oil in a middling temp. Include cut onion and crushed garlic, then cook 'til softened, about 2 minutes.
3. Place cut red bell pepper, julienned carrot, and julienned zucchini to your skillet. Cook for extra 3-4 minutes 'til vegetables are tender-crisp.
4. Stir in red curry paste then cook for 1 minute 'til fragrant.
5. Pour coconut milk into your skillet, along with fish sauce and brown sugar. Stir well to blend.
6. Include skinned and deveined shrimp to your skillet then cook for 5-6 minutes 'til shrimp are pink then cooked through.
7. Squeeze lime juice over the coconut curry shrimp then stir to blend.
8. Present coconut curry shrimp over cooked rice noodles, garnished using fresh cilantro. Relish!

Per serving: Calories: 604kcal; Fat: 26g; Carbs: 79g; Protein: 22g; Sugar: 11g; Sodium: 820mg; Potassium: 798mg; Glycemic index: 45

66. Baked Lemon Pepper Mahi Mahi

Recipe type:
Difficulty: Easy
Preparation time: 10 minutes
Cooking time: 15 minutes
Servings: 2
Ingredients:

- 2 mahi mahi fillets
- 2 tbsps. olive oil
- Zest and juice of 1 lemon
- 1 tsp. black pepper
- Salt as required
- Fresh parsley for garnish (optional)

Directions:

1. Warm up oven to 400 deg.F. Cover a baking sheet with parchment paper and put it away.
2. Place mahi mahi fillets on your organized baking sheet.
3. In your small bowl, blend olive oil, lemon zest, lemon juice, black pepper, and salt. Blend thoroughly.
4. Brush the lemon pepper mixture over the mahi mahi fillets, coating them uniformly.
5. Bake mahi mahi in to your warmed up oven for 12-15 minutes, or 'til fish flakes simply using a fork and is cooked through.
6. Garnish using fresh parsley if wanted and serve hot with your favorite side dishes. Relish!

Per serving: Calories: 265kcal; Fat: 14g; Carbs: 2g; Protein: 31g; Sugar: 0g; Sodium: 116mg; Potassium: 525mg; Glycemic index: 1

67. Lemon Herb Tilapia

Recipe type:
Difficulty: Easy
Preparation time: 10 minutes
Cooking time: 15 minutes
Servings: 2
Ingredients:

- 2 tilapia fillets
- 2 tbsps. olive oil
- 2 pieces garlic, crushed
- Zest and juice of 1 lemon
- 1 tsp. dried thyme
- Salt and pepper as required
- Fresh parsley for garnish (optional)

Directions:

1. Warm up oven to 375 deg.F. Line a baking dish using parchment paper.
2. Place tilapia fillets in your prepared baking dish.
3. In your small bowl, whisk collectively olive oil, crushed garlic, lemon zest, lemon juice, dried thyme, salt, and pepper.
4. Put the lemon herb mixture over the tilapia fillets, spreading it uniformly to coat.
5. Bake tilapia in to your warmed up oven for 12-15 minutes, or 'til fish flakes simply using a fork and is cooked through.
6. Garnish using fresh parsley if wanted and serve hot with your favorite side dishes. Relish!

Per serving: Calories: 243kcal; Fat: 14g; Carbs: 3g; Protein: 27g; Sugar: 0g; Sodium: 81mg; Potassium: 489mg; Glycemic index: 1

68. Seared Scallops with White Wine Sauce

Recipe type:
Difficulty: Hard
Preparation time: 20 minutes
Cooking time: 15 minutes
Servings: 2
Ingredients:

- 12 big scallops
- Salt and pepper as required
- 2 tbsps. olive oil
- 1/4 cup dry white wine
- 2 tbsps. unsalted butter
- 2 pieces garlic, crushed
- 1 tbsp. chopped fresh parsley
- Lemon wedges for presenting

Directions:

1. Pat scallops dry using paper towels and flavour them using salt and pepper on both sides.
2. Warm olive oil in a huge skillet in a med-high temp. 'til hot but not smoking.
3. Carefully include scallops to your skillet, making sure not to overcrowd them. Cook 2-3 minutes on all sides 'til golden brown and caramelized.
4. Take out cooked scallops from the skillet and transfer to a plate. Cover to keep warm.
5. In the same skillet, include dry white wine then deglaze the pan, scraping up any browned bits from the bottom.
6. Include unsalted butter and crushed garlic to your skillet. Cook for 2-3 minutes 'til garlic is fragrant and butter is melted.
7. Return scallops to your skillet then toss them in the white wine sauce to coat uniformly. Cook for extra minute 'til scallops are heated through.
8. Sprinkle chopped fresh parsley over the scallops and take out from heat.
9. Present seared scallops hot with lemon wedges on the side. Relish!

Per serving: Calories: 280kcal; Fat: 18g; Carbs: 4g; Protein: 19g; Sugar: 0g; Sodium: 626mg; Potassium: 454mg; Glycemic index: 0

Side Dishes Recipes

69. Quinoa Pilaf with Vegetables

Recipe type:
Difficulty: Easy
Preparation time: 15 minutes
Cooking time: 15 minutes
Servings: 2
Ingredients:

- 1/2 cup quinoa
- 1 cup vegetable broth
- 1 tbsp. olive oil
- 1/4 cup diced onion
- 1/4 cup diced bell pepper
- 1/4 cup diced zucchini
- 1/4 cup diced carrot
- 1 clove garlic, crushed
- Salt and pepper as required
- 2 tbsps. chopped fresh parsley (optional)

Directions:

1. Rinse quinoa under cold water and drain well.
2. In your saucepan, bring vegetable broth to a boil. Include quinoa, decrease temp. to low, cover, then simmer for 12-15 minutes 'til liquid is immersed and quinoa is tender.
3. In your skillet, warm olive oil in a middling temp. Include diced onion, bell pepper, zucchini, carrot, and crushed garlic. Cook for 5-6 minutes 'til vegetables are tender.
4. Fluff cooked quinoa using a fork and transfer to your skillet with the cooked vegetables. Stir well to blend.
5. Flavour quinoa pilaf using salt and pepper as required. Garnish using chopped fresh parsley, if wanted.
6. Present hot as a side dish. Relish!

Per serving: Calories: 237kcal; Fat: 9g; Carbs: 33g; Protein: 7g; Sugar: 4g; Sodium: 427mg; Potassium: 496mg; Glycemic index: 13

70. Eggplant Caponata

Recipe type:
Difficulty: Medium
Preparation time: 15 minutes
Cooking time: 30 minutes
Servings: 2
Ingredients:

- 1 medium eggplant, diced
- 1 onion, diced
- 2 pieces garlic, crushed
- 1 can (14 oz) diced tomatoes, drained
- 2 tbsps. capers
- 2 tbsps. red wine vinegar
- 1 tbsp. honey
- 1/4 cup chopped fresh basil
- Salt and pepper as required
- Olive oil for cooking

Directions:

1. Warm olive oil in a huge skillet in a middling temp. Include diced eggplant and diced onion, then cook 'til softened, around 5-7 minutes.
2. Include crushed garlic to your skillet then cook for extra 1-2 minutes 'til fragrant.
3. Stir in drained diced tomatoes, capers, red wine vinegar, and honey. Cook for 15-20 minutes, mixing irregularly, 'til eggplant is tender and mixture is mildly thickened.
4. Flavour using salt and pepper as required, then stir in chopped fresh basil.
5. Take out from heat and transfer to a serving dish.
6. Present warm or at room temp. Relish!

Per serving: Calories: 183kcal; Fat: 2g; Carbs: 42g; Protein: 5g; Sugar: 28g; Sodium: 338mg; Potassium: 1070mg; Glycemic index: 40

71. Asparagus Risotto with Parmesan Cheese

Recipe type:
Difficulty: Hard
Preparation time: 10 minutes
Cooking time: 30 minutes
Servings: 2
Ingredients:

- 1 cup Arborio rice
- 3 cups vegetable broth
- 1 bunch asparagus, cut into 1" pieces
- 1 onion, finely chopped
- 2 pieces garlic, crushed
- 1/2 cup grated Parmesan cheese
- 1/4 cup dry white wine (optional)
- 2 tbsps. unsalted butter
- 1 tbsp. olive oil
- Salt and pepper as required
- Fresh parsley leaves for garnish (optional)

Directions:

1. In your saucepan, bring vegetable broth to a simmer then keep it warm over low heat.
2. In your distinct big skillet, warm olive oil in a middling temp. Include finely chopped onion and crushed garlic, then cook 'til softened, around 3-4 minutes.
3. Include Arborio rice to your skillet then cook for 1-2 minutes 'til rice is coated with oil and mildly toasted.
4. If using white wine, pour it into your skillet then cook 'til it is immersed by the rice, mixing regularly.
5. Begin adding warm vegetable broth to your skillet, one ladleful at a time, mixing regularly and letting the broth to be immersed before including extra. Continue this process 'til the rice is creamy then cooked al dente, around 20-25 minutes.
6. In the last 5 minutes of cooking, stir in trimmed asparagus pieces and continue cooking 'til asparagus is tender-crisp.
7. Stir in grated Parmesan cheese and unsalted butter 'til well blended. Flavour using salt and pepper as required.
8. Take out from heat then let it rest for a couple of minutes prior to presenting.
9. Garnish using fresh parsley leaves, if wanted. Relish!

Per serving: Calories: 703kcal; Fat: 26g; Carbs: 85g; Protein: 21g; Sugar: 6g; Sodium: 1379mg; Potassium: 819mg; Glycemic index: 55

72. Brown Rice with Peas and Carrots

Recipe type:
Difficulty: Easy
Preparation time: 5 minutes
Cooking time: 30 minutes
Servings: 2
Ingredients:

- 1/2 cup brown rice
- 1 cup water
- 1/2 cup frozen peas
- 1/2 cup diced carrots
- Salt and pepper as required

Directions:

1. Rinse brown rice under cold water and drain well.
2. In your saucepan, bring water to a boil. Include brown rice, decrease temp. to low, cover, then simmer for 25-30 minutes 'til rice is tender and water is immersed.
3. In the last 5 minutes of cooking, include frozen peas and diced carrots to the saucepan with the cooking rice. Cover and continue cooking 'til vegetables are tender.

4. Once rice and vegetables are cooked, fluff the rice using a fork and flavour using salt and pepper as required.
5. Transfer to a serving dish then serve hot. Relish!

Per serving: Calories: 139kcal; Fat: 1g; Carbs: 29g; Protein: 4g; Sugar: 2g; Sodium: 15mg; Potassium: 262mg; Glycemic index: 50

73. Sautéed Spinach with Garlic and Lemon

Recipe type:
Difficulty: Easy
Preparation time: 5 minutes
Cooking time: 5 minutes
Servings: 2
Ingredients:

- 8 oz fresh spinach leaves
- 2 pieces garlic, crushed
- 1 tbsp. olive oil
- Juice of 1/2 lemon
- Salt and pepper as required

Directions:

1. Warm olive oil in a huge skillet in a middling temp. Include crushed garlic then cook for 1-2 minutes 'til fragrant.
2. Include fresh spinach leaves to your skillet then cook for 2-3 minutes, tossing occasionally, 'til wilted.
3. Squeeze lemon juice over the sautéed spinach and flavour using salt and pepper as required. Toss to blend.
4. Take out from heat and transfer to a serving dish. Present hot. Relish!

Per serving: Calories: 86kcal; Fat: 7g; Carbs: 5g; Protein: 3g; Sugar: 0g; Sodium: 88mg; Potassium: 738mg; Glycemic index: 15

74. Potato Leek Gratin with Gruyere Cheese

Recipe type:
Difficulty: Hard
Preparation time: 20 minutes
Cooking time: 1 hour
Servings: 2
Ingredients:

- 2 big potatoes, skinned and finely cut
- 2 leeks, white and light green parts, cut
- 1 cup shredded Gruyere cheese
- 1 cup heavy cream
- 2 pieces garlic, crushed
- 2 tbsps. unsalted butter
- Salt and pepper as required
- Fresh thyme leaves for garnish (optional)

Directions:

1. Warm up oven to 375 deg.F. Grease a baking dish with butter.
2. In your skillet, melt unsalted butter in a middling temp. Include crushed garlic then cut leeks, then cook 'til softened, around 5-7 minutes.
3. Organize a layer of your finely cut potatoes in the bottom of the prepared baking dish. Top with half of the cooked leek mixture and half of the shredded Gruyere cheese.
4. Repeat the layers using the rest of the potatoes, leek mixture, and Gruyere cheese.
5. In your small saucepan, heat heavy cream in a middling temp. 'til warmed through. Flavour using salt and pepper as required.
6. Put the warmed heavy cream uniformly over the potato and leek layers in the baking dish.
7. Cover the baking dish using foil and bake in to your warmed up oven for 45 minutes.

8. Take out the foil and bake for extra 15 minutes, or 'til the top is golden brown and the potatoes are tender.
9. Let it cool for a couple of minutes prior to presenting.
10. Garnish using fresh thyme leaves, if wanted. Relish!

Per serving: Calories: 762kcal; Fat: 56g; Carbs: 42g; Protein: 29g; Sugar: 7g; Sodium: 369mg; Potassium: 1360mg; Glycemic index: 10

75. Garlic Roasted Green Beans

Recipe type:
Difficulty: Easy
Preparation time: 10 minutes
Cooking time: 15 minutes
Servings: 2
Ingredients:

- 1/2 lb fresh green beans, trimmed
- 2 tbsps. olive oil
- 2 pieces garlic, crushed
- Salt and pepper as required

Directions:

1. Warm up oven to 400 deg.F. Cover a baking sheet with parchment paper and put it away.
2. In your bowl, toss green beans using olive oil, crushed garlic, salt, and pepper 'til uniformly covered.
3. Disperse seasoned green beans in a one layer on your organized baking sheet.
4. Roast green beans in to your warmed up oven for 12-15 minutes, or 'til tender and mildly caramelized, mixing halfway through cooking.
5. Take out from the oven and transfer to a serving dish. Present hot. Relish!

Per serving: Calories: 138kcal; Fat: 11g; Carbs: 10g; Protein: 2g; Sugar: 3g; Sodium: 8mg; Potassium: 239mg; Glycemic index: 15

76. Grilled Corn on the Cob with Lime Cilantro Butter

Recipe type:
Difficulty: Medium
Preparation time: 10 minutes
Cooking time: 15 minutes
Servings: 2
Ingredients:

- 2 ears of corn, husked
- 2 tbsps. unsalted butter, softened
- 1 tbsp. chopped fresh cilantro
- Zest of 1 lime
- Juice of 1/2 lime
- Salt and pepper as required

Directions:

1. Warm up grill to med-high temp.
2. In your small bowl, blend softened unsalted butter, chopped fresh cilantro, lime zest, lime juice, salt, and pepper to make the lime cilantro butter.
3. Disperse lime cilantro butter uniformly over each ear of corn.
4. Place corn on the warmed up grill then cook for 10-15 minutes, turning occasionally, 'til kernels are tender and mildly charred.
5. Take out grilled corn from the grill and transfer to a serving plate.
6. Present hot. Relish!

Per serving: Calories: 166kcal; Fat: 11g; Carbs: 19g; Protein: 3g; Sugar: 6g; Sodium: 11mg; Potassium: 243mg; Glycemic index: 20

Sweets Recipes

77. Lemon Poppy Seed Muffins with Whole Wheat Flour

Recipe type:
Difficulty: Medium
Preparation time: 15 minutes
Cooking time: 20-25 minutes
Servings: 2 (6 muffins each)
Ingredients:

- 1 cup whole wheat flour
- 1/2 cup almond flour
- 1/4 cup honey or maple syrup
- 1/4 cup unsweetened applesauce
- 1/4 cup Greek yogurt
- 1/4 cup almond milk
- 1/4 cup coconut oil, melted
- Juice and zest of 1 lemon
- 2 tbsps. poppy seeds
- 1 tsp. baking powder
- 1/2 tsp. baking soda
- Pinch of salt

Directions:

1. Warm up your oven to 350 deg.F. Line a muffin tin using paper liners or oil it with coconut oil.
2. In your big mixing bowl, blend whole wheat flour, almond flour, honey or maple syrup, unsweetened applesauce, Greek yogurt, almond milk, melted coconut oil, lemon juice and zest, poppy seeds, baking powder, baking soda, and a pinch of salt. Mix 'til just blended.
3. Spoon the muffin batter in to your prepared muffin tin, filling each cup 3/4 full.
4. Bake in to your warmed up oven for 20-25 minutes, or up until the point where a toothpick that is placed into the middle of a muffin comes out clean.
5. Take out the muffins from the oven then let them cool in the tin for a couple of minutes before placing to your wire rack to cool entirely.
6. Relish these delightful lemon poppy seed muffins as a wholesome breakfast or snack!

Per serving: Calories: 233kcal; Fat: 12g; Carbs: 29g; Protein: 5g; Sugar: 13g; Sodium: 119mg; Potassium: 127mg; Glycemic index: 55

78. Grilled Pineapple w/ Honey and Mint

Recipe type:
Difficulty: Easy
Preparation time: 10 minutes
Cooking time: 5 minutes · **Servings:** 2
Ingredients:

- 1 ripe pineapple, skinned, cored, then cut into rings
- 2 tbsps. honey
- Fresh mint leaves for garnish

Directions:

1. Warm up grill to med-high temp.
2. Place pineapple rings on the warmed up grill then cook for around 2-3 minutes on all sides, or 'til grill marks appear and pineapple is mildly caramelized.
3. Take out grilled pineapple from the grill and transfer to a serving platter.
4. Drizzle honey over the grilled pineapple slices.
5. Garnish using fresh mint leaves and serve instantly as a delightful dessert or snack.

Per serving: Calories: 169kcal; Fat: 0g; Carbs: 45g; Protein: 1g; Sugar: 38g; Sodium: 2mg; Potassium: 281mg; Glycemic index: 40

79. Baked Pear Crisp with Oat Topping

Recipe type:
Difficulty: Medium
Preparation time: 15 minutes
Cooking time: 35-40 minutes
Servings: 2
Ingredients:

For the pear filling:

- 3 ripe pears, skinned, cored, then cut
- 2 tbsps. honey or maple syrup
- 1 tbsp. lemon juice
- 1/2 tsp. ground cinnamon
- 1/4 tsp. ground nutmeg
- Pinch of salt

For the oat topping:

- 1/2 cup rolled oats
- 1/4 cup almond flour
- 2 tbsps. coconut oil or an unsalted butter (melted)
- 2 tbsps. honey or maple syrup
- 1/4 tsp. ground cinnamon
- Pinch of salt

Directions:

1. Warm up your oven to 350 deg.F. Grease a small baking dish or two ramekins and put away.
2. In your mixing bowl, blend cut pears, honey or maple syrup, lemon juice, ground cinnamon, ground nutmeg, and a pinch of salt. Toss 'til the pears are uniformly covered.
3. Put the pear mixture to the prepared baking dish or ramekins, dispersing it out uniformly.
4. In your another mixing bowl, blend rolled oats, almond flour, melted coconut oil or butter, honey or maple syrup, ground cinnamon, then a pinch of salt. Mix 'til the mixture resembles coarse crumbs.
5. Afterward, spread the oat topping over the pear filling uniformly.
6. Bake in to your warmed up oven for 35-40 minutes, or 'til the pear filling is bubbling and the oat topping is golden brown.
7. Take out from the oven then let it cool for a couple of minutes prior to presenting.
8. Present warm with a scoop of your vanilla ice cream or a dollop of your Greek yogurt, if wanted. Relish this delicious baked pear crisp!

Per serving: Calories: 275kcal; Fat: 10g; Carbs: 48g; Protein: 4g; Sugar: 29g; Sodium: 80mg; Potassium: 279mg; Glycemic index: 55

80. Coconut Milk Rice Pudding with Mango

Recipe type:
Difficulty: Hard
Preparation time: 10 minutes
Cooking time: 45-50 minutes
Servings: 2
Ingredients:

- 1/2 cup arborio rice
- 2 cups coconut milk
- 1/4 cup honey or maple syrup
- 1 tsp. vanilla extract
- Pinch of salt
- 1 ripe mango, skinned, pitted, and diced
- Toasted coconut flakes for garnish (optional)

Directions:

1. In your saucepan, blend arborio rice, coconut milk, honey or maple syrup, vanilla extract, and a pinch of salt. Stir well.
2. Simmer the mixture in a middling temp., then decrease the temp. to low then cook, mixing irregularly, for 45-50 minutes, or 'til the rice is tender and the mixture is creamy.
3. Take out the rice pudding from the heat then let it cool mildly.
4. Once the rice pudding has cooled, transfer it to serving bowls or glasses.
5. Chill the rice pudding in the fridge for almost 2 hours, or 'til cold.
6. Before serving, top the chilled rice pudding with your diced mango and toasted coconut flakes, if wanted.
7. Relish this creamy and tropical coconut milk rice pudding with mango as a delightful dessert!

Per serving: Calories: 483kcal; Fat: 24g; Carbs: 65g; Protein: 4g; Sugar: 36g; Sodium: 105mg; Potassium: 466mg; Glycemic index: 55

81. Mango Sorbet

Recipe type:
Difficulty: Easy
Preparation time: 5 minutes
Cooking time: 0 minutes
Servings: 2
Ingredients:

- 2 ripe mangoes, skinned, pitted, and diced
- 1 tbsp. lime juice
- 2 tbsps. honey or maple syrup (sweeteners)
- Fresh mint leaves for garnish (optional)

Directions:

1. Place diced mangoes in a mixer or blending container. Include honey or maple syrup (if using) and lime juice.
2. Blend 'til smooth and creamy.
3. Put the mango mixture into a shallow dish or baking pan.
4. Cover using plastic wrap or foil and freeze for almost 4 hours, or 'til firm.
5. Once frozen, take out the mango mixture from the freezer then let it sit at room temp. for a couple of minutes to soften mildly.
6. Scoop the mango sorbet into serving bowls or glasses.
7. Garnish using fresh mint leaves, if wanted, and serve instantly.

Per serving: Calories: 161kcal; Fat: 1g; Carbs: 42g; Protein: 2g; Sugar: 38g; Sodium: 3mg; Potassium: 415mg; Glycemic index: 40

82. Baked Apples with Cinnamon and Walnuts

Recipe type:
Difficulty: Easy
Preparation time: 10 minutes
Cooking time: 30 minutes
Servings: 2
Ingredients:

- 2 apples (e.g., Granny Smith or Honeycrisp)
- 1 tbsp. lemon juice
- 1 tbsp. chopped walnuts
- 1 tbsp. raisins (optional)
- 1/2 tsp. ground cinnamon
- 1/2 tsp. nutmeg
- Honey or maple syrup (optional, for drizzling)

Directions:

1. Warm up oven to 375 deg.F. Line a baking dish using parchment paper.
2. Core the apples then slice off the top to create a cavity for the filling. Put the apples in your prepared baking dish.
3. Drizzle your lemon juice over the apples to prevent browning.
4. In your small bowl, blend collectively chopped walnuts, raisins (if using), ground cinnamon, and nutmeg.
5. Stuff each apple with the walnut mixture, pressing gently to fill the cavity.
6. Bake in to your warmed up oven for 25-30 minutes, or 'til the apples are tender and mildly golden brown.
7. Take out from the oven then let them cool for a couple of minutes prior to presenting.
8. Drizzle honey or maple syrup over the baked apples, if wanted.
9. Present warm as a delightful dessert or snack.

Per serving: Calories: 177kcal; Fat: 4g; Carbs: 39g; Protein: 1g; Sugar: 29g; Sodium: 3mg; Potassium: 298mg; Glycemic index: 40

83. Dark Chocolate Covered Strawberries

Recipe type:
Difficulty: Easy
Preparation time: 10 minutes
Cooking time: 0 minutes
Servings: 2 (6 strawberries each)
Ingredients:

- 12 fresh strawberries
- 1/4 cup dark chocolate chips
- 1 tsp. coconut oil (optional)

Directions:

1. Wash the strawberries then pat them dry using a paper towel. Make sure they are entirely dry before dipping.
2. In your microwave-safe bowl, melt the dark chocolate chips in your microwave in 30-second intervals, mixing between each interval 'til smooth. Stir in coconut oil, if using, to thin out the chocolate.
3. Hold each strawberry by the stem and dip it into the melted chocolate, coating it halfway.
4. Put your chocolate-covered strawberries on a parchment-lined baking sheet.
5. Refrigerate for around 10-15 minutes, or 'til the chocolate is set.
6. Present these elegant and indulgent dark chocolate covered strawberries as a delightful dessert or romantic treat.

Per serving: Calories: 115kcal; Fat: 6g; Carbs: 17g; Protein: 2g; Sugar: 9g; Sodium: 1mg; Potassium: 173mg; Glycemic index: 40

84. Berry Tart with Almond Flour Crust

Recipe type:
Difficulty: Hard
Preparation time: 30 minutes
Cooking time: 20-25 minutes
Servings: 2
Ingredients:

For the almond flour crust:

- 1 1/2 cups almond flour
- 1/4 cup coconut oil, melted
- 2 tbsps. honey or maple syrup
- 1/2 tsp. vanilla extract
- Pinch of salt

For the berry filling:

- 2 cups mixed berries (e.g., strawberries, blueberries, raspberries)
- 2 tbsps. honey or maple syrup
- 1 tbsp. cornstarch
- Juice of 1/2 lemon

Directions:

1. Warm up your oven to 350 deg.F. Grease a 9-inch tart pan with a removable bottom and put away.
2. In your mixing bowl, blend melted coconut oil, almond flour, honey or maple syrup, vanilla extract, and a pinch of salt. Mix 'til the mixture resembles coarse crumbs and sticks together when pressed.
3. Press the almond flour mixture uniformly into the bottom then up the sides of the prepared tart pan.
4. Bake the almond flour crust in to your warmed up oven for 20-25 minutes, or 'til golden brown.
5. While crust is baking, prepare the berry filling. In your saucepan, blend mixed berries, honey or maple syrup, cornstarch, and lemon juice. Cook in a middling temp., mixing irregularly, 'til the berries soften and release their juices, and the mixture thickens.
6. Once crust is baked, take out it from the oven then let it cool entirely.
7. Put the berry filling into the cooled almond flour crust, dispersing it out uniformly.
8. Chill the berry tart in the fridge for almost 2 hours prior to presenting.
9. Slice and serve this delightful berry tart with almond flour crust as a decadent dessert!

Per serving: Calories: 512kcal; Fat: 38g; Carbs: 40g; Protein: 10g; Sugar: 24g; Sodium: 68mg; Potassium: 312mg; Glycemic index: 40

85. Avocado Chocolate Mousse

Recipe type:

Difficulty: Medium

Preparation time: 10 minutes

Cooking time: 0 minutes

Servings: 2

Ingredients:

- 1 ripe avocado, skinned and pitted
- 1/4 cup unsweetened cocoa powder
- 1/4 cup honey or maple syrup
- 1 tsp. vanilla extract
- Pinch of salt
- Fresh berries for garnish (optional)

Directions:

1. In your blending container or blender, blend ripe avocado, cocoa powder, honey or maple syrup, vanilla extract, and a pinch of salt. Blend 'til smooth and creamy.
2. Taste the mousse and adjust sweetness if needed by including extra honey or maple syrup.
3. Put the avocado chocolate mousse to serving glasses or bowls.
4. Cover, put in the fridge for 1 hour to chill and set.
5. Before serving, garnish using fresh berries, if wanted.
6. Relish this creamy and indulgent avocado chocolate mousse as a guilt-free dessert!

Per serving: Calories: 248kcal; Fat: 15g; Carbs: 33g; Protein: 4g; Sugar: 23g; Sodium: 9mg; Potassium: 571mg; Glycemic index: 40

86. Frozen Banana Bites with Peanut Butter

Recipe type:

Difficulty: Easy

Preparation time: 10 minutes

Cooking time: 0 minutes

Servings: 2

Ingredients:

- 1 ripe banana
- 2 tbsps. peanut butter
- 1/4 cup dark chocolate chips (optional)

Directions:

1. Peel the banana and cut it into bite-sized slices.
2. Disperse a small amount of your peanut butter onto one side of each banana slice.
3. If using dark chocolate chips, melt them in your microwave in 30-second intervals, mixing between each interval 'til smooth.
4. Dip each peanut butter-coated banana slice into the melted dark chocolate, coating half of the slice.
5. Put the banana bites on a parchment-lined baking sheet.
6. Freeze for almost 1 hour, or 'til firm.
7. Once frozen, take out the banana bites from the freezer then let them sit at room temp. for a couple of minutes prior to presenting.
8. Present these delightful frozen banana bites as a guilt-free treat or snack.

Per serving: Calories: 240kcal; Fat: 14g; Carbs: 27g; Protein: 5g; Sugar: 15g; Sodium: 78mg; Potassium: 362mg; Glycemic index: 40

Instant Pot Recipes

87. Black Bean and Sweet Potato Chili

Recipe type:
Difficulty: Easy
Preparation time: 10 minutes
Cooking time: 25 minutes
Servings: 2
Ingredients:

- 1 tbsp. olive oil
- 1 onion, diced
- 2 pieces garlic, crushed
- 1 sweet potato, skinned and diced
- 1 bell pepper, diced
- 1 can (15 oz.) black beans
- 1 can (14.5 oz.) diced tomatoes
- 1 cup low-sodium vegetable broth
- 1 tsp. chili powder
- 1/2 tsp. cumin
- Salt and pepper as required

Directions:

1. Adjust Instant Pot to sauté mode and warm olive oil.
2. Include diced onion and crushed garlic, sauté 'til fragrant.
3. Include diced sweet potato and bell pepper, cook for extra 3-4 minutes.
4. Stir in black beans, diced tomatoes, vegetable broth, chili powder, and cumin.
5. Put the lid back on and adjust the valve so that it is in the sealing position.
6. Cook on high pressure for 15 minutes.
7. After the cooking cycle has been completed, allow the pressure to dissipate completely naturally for 5 minutes, and then quickly and cautiously release rest of the pressure.
8. Open the lid and flavour the chili using salt and pepper as required.
9. Present the black bean and sweet potato chili hot.

Per serving: Calories: 340kcal; Fat: 6g; Carbs: 63g; Protein: 14g; Sugar: 13g; Sodium: 689mg; Potassium: 1240mg; Glycemic index: 30

88. Stuffed Acorn Squash with Quinoa and Cranberries

Recipe type:
Difficulty: Hard
Preparation time: 30 minutes
Cooking time: 25 minutes
Servings: 2
Ingredients:

- 1 acorn squash, divided and seeds taken out
- 1/2 cup quinoa, washed
- 1 cup vegetable broth
- 1/4 cup dried cranberries
- 1/4 cup chopped pecans
- 1 tbsp. olive oil
- 1/2 onion, diced
- 1 celery stalk, diced
- 1 carrot, diced
- 1/2 tsp. ground cinnamon
- Salt and pepper as required

Directions:

1. Put the acorn squash halves cut-side down in the Instant Pot.
2. Place 1 cup of water to the Instant Pot.
3. Close the lid then set the valve to the sealing position.
4. Cook on high pressure for 5 minutes.
5. Once the cooking cycle is complete, carefully quick release the pressure.
6. Take out the acorn squash halves from the Instant Pot and put away.

7. Rinse the Instant Pot insert and dry it thoroughly.
8. Adjust Instant Pot to sauté mode and warm olive oil.
9. Include diced onion, diced celery, and diced carrot, sauté 'til softened.
10. Stir in washed quinoa, vegetable broth, dried cranberries, chopped pecans, ground cinnamon, salt, and pepper.
11. Put the cooked acorn squash halves back into the Instant Pot, cut-side up.
12. Stuff each acorn squash half using the quinoa mixture.
13. Put the lid back on and adjust the valve so that it is in the sealing position.
14. Cook on high pressure for 10 minutes.
15. After the cooking cycle has been completed, allow the pressure to dissipate completely naturally for 5 minutes, and then quickly and cautiously release rest of the pressure.
16. Open the lid and serve the filled acorn squash hot.

Per serving: Calories: 413kcal; Fat: 14g; Carbs: 68g; Protein: 10g; Sugar: 18g; Sodium: 617mg; Potassium: 1346mg; Glycemic index: 55

89. Chicken and Vegetable Paella

Recipe type:
Difficulty: Hard
Preparation time: 30 minutes
Cooking time: 15 minutes
Servings: 2
Ingredients:

- 2 boneless, skinless chicken thighs, bite-sized pieces
- 1 onion, diced
- 2 pieces garlic, crushed
- 1 bell pepper, diced
- 1 tomato, diced
- 1 cup Arborio rice
- 2 cups low-sodium chicken broth
- 1/2 cup frozen peas
- 1/4 tsp. saffron threads
- 1/2 tsp. smoked paprika
- Salt and pepper as required
- Lemon wedges for presenting (optional)
- Chopped fresh parsley for garnish (optional)

Directions:

1. Adjust Instant Pot to sauté mode and warm olive oil.
2. Include diced onion and crushed garlic, sauté 'til fragrant.
3. Include diced bell pepper and diced tomato, cook for extra 2-3 minutes.
4. Include chicken pieces then cook 'til browned on all sides.
5. Stir in Arborio rice, saffron threads, smoked paprika, salt, and pepper.
6. Pour low-sodium chicken broth into the Instant Pot then stir well to blend.
7. Put the lid back on and adjust the valve so that it is in the sealing position.
8. Cook on high pressure for 5 minutes.
9. After the cooking cycle has been completed, allow the pressure to dissipate completely naturally for 5 minutes, and then quickly and cautiously release rest of the pressure.
10. Open the lid then stir in frozen peas.
11. Present the chicken and vegetable paella hot, garnished using chopped fresh parsley and lemon wedges if wanted.

Per serving: Calories: 541kcal; Fat: 11g; Carbs: 84g; Protein: 30g; Sugar: 8g; Sodium: 251mg; Potassium: 859mg; Glycemic index: 50

90. Lentil and Vegetable Curry

Recipe type:
Difficulty: Easy
Preparation time: 10 minutes
Cooking time: 20 minutes
Servings: 2
Ingredients:

- 1 cup dried lentils, washed
- 2 cups vegetable broth
- 1 onion, diced
- 2 pieces garlic, crushed
- 1 bell pepper, diced
- 1 zucchini, diced
- 1 can (14.5 oz.) diced tomatoes
- 2 tbsps. curry powder
- 1 tsp. ground cumin
- Salt as required
- Fresh cilantro for garnish (optional)

Directions:

1. In the Instant Pot, blend dried lentils, vegetable broth, diced onion, crushed garlic, diced bell pepper, diced zucchini, diced tomatoes, curry powder, and ground cumin.
2. Stir everything together 'til well blended.
3. Put the lid back on and adjust the valve so that it is in the sealing position.
4. Cook on high pressure for 15 minutes.
5. After the cooking cycle has been completed, allow the pressure to dissipate completely naturally for 5 minutes, and then quickly and cautiously release rest of the pressure.
6. Open the lid then stir the lentil and vegetable curry.
7. Flavour with salt as required.
8. Present hot, garnished using fresh cilantro if wanted.

Per serving: Calories: 343kcal; Fat: 2g; Carbs: 64g; Protein: 22g; Sugar: 13g; Sodium: 707mg; Potassium: 1341mg; Glycemic index: 11

91. Ratatouille with Chickpeas

Recipe type:
Difficulty: Easy
Preparation time: 15 minutes
Cooking time: 15 minutes
Servings: 2
Ingredients:

- 1 tbsp. olive oil
- 1 onion, diced
- 2 pieces garlic, crushed
- 1 eggplant, diced
- 1 zucchini, diced
- 1 yellow bell pepper, diced
- 1 can (14.5 oz.) diced tomatoes
- 1 can (15 oz.) chickpeas
- 1 tsp. dried thyme
- 1 tsp. dried oregano
- Salt and pepper as required
- Fresh basil for garnish (optional)

Directions:

1. Adjust Instant Pot to sauté mode and warm olive oil.
2. Include diced onion and crushed garlic, sauté 'til fragrant.
3. Include diced eggplant, diced zucchini, and diced yellow bell pepper, cook for 5-7 minutes 'til mildly softened.
4. Stir in diced tomatoes, chickpeas, dried thyme, and dried oregano.
5. Put the lid back on and adjust the valve so that it is in the sealing position.
6. Cook on high pressure for 5 minutes.

7. After the cooking cycle has been completed, allow the pressure to dissipate completely naturally for 5 minutes, and then quickly and cautiously release rest of the pressure.
8. Open the lid and flavour the ratatouille using salt and pepper as required.
9. Present hot, garnished using fresh basil if wanted.

Per serving: Calories: 380kcal; Fat: 10g; Carbs: 63g; Protein: 16g; Sugar: 16g; Sodium: 884mg; Potassium: 1488mg; Glycemic index: 19

92. Mediterranean Quinoa Salad

Recipe type:
Difficulty: Easy
Preparation time: 10 minutes
Cooking time: 1 minute (for quinoa)
Servings: 2
Ingredients:

- 1/2 cup quinoa, washed
- 1 cup water
- 1 cup cherry tomatoes, divided
- 1/2 cucumber, diced
- 1/4 cup Kalamata olives
- 1/4 cup chopped fresh parsley
- 2 tbsps. extra virgin olive oil
- 1 tbsp. lemon juice
- 1 clove garlic, crushed
- Salt and pepper as required

Directions:

1. In the Instant Pot, blend quinoa and water.
2. Put the lid back on and adjust the valve so that it is in the sealing position.
3. Cook on high pressure for 1 minute.
4. Once the cooking cycle is complete, let for a natural pressure release to 10 minutes, then carefully quick release rest of the pressure.
5. Fluff the quinoa using a fork and transfer it to a big mixing bowl.
6. Include cherry tomatoes, cucumber, Kalamata olives, and chopped parsley to the bowl with quinoa.
7. In your small bowl, whisk collectively extra virgin olive oil, lemon juice, crushed garlic, salt, and pepper.
8. Put the dressing over the quinoa salad then toss 'til well blended.
9. Present the Mediterranean quinoa salad instantly or put in the fridge 'til ready to serve.

Per serving: Calories: 293kcal; Fat: 15g; Carbs: 32g; Protein: 7g; Sugar: 3g; Sodium: 310mg; Potassium: 510mg; Glycemic index: 13

93. Quinoa and Black Bean Stuffed Peppers

Recipe type: 🌱🌿🚫🌾
Difficulty: Medium
Preparation time: 20 minutes
Cooking time: 10 minutes
Servings: 2
Ingredients:

- 2 big bell peppers, divided and seeds taken out
- 1/2 cup quinoa, washed
- 1 cup water
- 1 can (15 oz.) black beans
- 1/2 cup corn kernels
- 1/2 cup diced tomatoes
- 1/2 tsp. ground cumin
- 1/2 tsp. chili powder
- Salt and pepper as required
- Fresh cilantro for garnish (optional)
- Lime wedges for presenting (optional)

Directions:

1. In your small saucepan, blend quinoa and water. oil, then decrease temp., cover, then simmer for 15 minutes 'til quinoa is cooked and water is immersed.
2. Warm up the Instant Pot using the sauté mode.
3. In your bowl, blend collectively cooked quinoa, black beans, corn kernels, diced tomatoes, ground cumin, chili powder, salt, and pepper.
4. Stuff the divided bell peppers with the quinoa and black bean mixture.
5. Put the filled bell peppers in the Instant Pot.
6. Close the lid then set the valve to the sealing position.
7. Cook on high pressure for 5 minutes.
8. After the cooking cycle has been completed, allow the pressure to dissipate completely naturally for 5 minutes, and then quickly and cautiously release rest of the pressure.
9. Open the lid and serve the quinoa and black bean filled peppers hot.
10. Garnish using fresh cilantro and serve with lime wedges if wanted.

Per serving: Calories: 395kcal; Fat: 3g; Carbs: 75g; Protein: 18g; Sugar: 8g; Sodium: 796mg; Potassium: 1212mg; Glycemic index: 13

Air Fryer Recipes

94. Harissa Spiced Chicken Thighs

Recipe type:
Difficulty: Hard
Preparation time: 15 minutes
Cooking time: 25 minutes
Servings: 2
Ingredients:

- 4 bone-in, skin-on chicken thighs
- 2 tbsps. harissa paste
- 1 tbsp. olive oil
- 1 tsp. smoked paprika
- 1/2 tsp. ground cumin
- 1/2 tsp. ground coriander
- Salt and pepper as required
- Lemon wedges for presenting (optional)

Directions:

1. In your bowl, blend collectively harissa paste, olive oil, smoked paprika, ground cumin, ground coriander, salt, and pepper.
2. Pat chicken thighs dry with paper towels.
3. Rub the harissa spice mixture all over the chicken thighs, ensuring they are uniformly covered.
4. Warm up the air fryer to 375 deg.F.
5. Put the chicken thighs in your air fryer basket, skin side down.
6. Cook for 15 minutes.
7. Flip the chicken thighs, skin side up, then cook for extra 10 minutes 'til the skin is crispy then the chicken is cooked through.
8. Present hot, with lemon wedges if wanted.

Per serving: Calories: 355kcal; Fat: 24g; Carbs: 3g; Protein: 30g; Sugar: 0g; Sodium: 303mg; Potassium: 393mg; Glycemic index: 12

95. Air Fryer Veggie Tacos

Recipe type:
Difficulty: Easy
Preparation time: 15 minutes
Cooking time: 10 minutes
Servings: 2
Ingredients:

- 4 small corn tortillas
- 1 cup mixed vegetables (e.g., onions, bell peppers, zucchini), cut
- 1 tbsp. olive oil
- 1 tsp. chili powder
- 1/2 tsp. ground cumin
- 1/2 tsp. garlic powder
- Salt and pepper as required
- Toppings of choice (e.g., salsa, avocado, cilantro, lime wedges)

Directions:

1. Warm up the air fryer to 375 deg.F.
2. In your bowl, toss mixed vegetables using olive oil, chili powder, ground cumin, garlic powder, salt, and pepper 'til uniformly covered.
3. Put the seasoned mixed vegetables in your air fryer basket.
4. Cook for 8-10 minutes, shaking the basket halfway through cooking, 'til the vegetables are tender and mildly charred.
5. In the meantime, warm your corn tortillas in the air fryer for 1-2 minutes.
6. Fill each tortilla with the cooked mixed vegetables.
7. Present the veggie tacos hot, with toppings of choice.

Per serving: Calories: 186kcal; Fat: 8g; Carbs: 25g; Protein: 4g; Sugar: 2g; Sodium: 173mg; Potassium: 248mg; Glycemic index: 52

96. Ratatouille Stuffed Bell Peppers

Recipe type:
Difficulty: Hard
Preparation time: 25 minutes
Cooking time: 30 minutes
Servings: 2
Ingredients:

- 2 big bell peppers, divided (seeds taken out)
- 1 small eggplant, diced
- 1 zucchini, diced
- 1 yellow squash, diced
- 1 red bell pepper, diced
- 1 onion, diced
- 2 pieces garlic, crushed
- 1 can (14 oz) diced tomatoes
- 1 tsp. dried thyme
- 1 tsp. dried basil
- Salt and pepper as required
- Olive oil for drizzling

Directions:

1. Warm up the air fryer to 375 deg.F.
2. In your skillet, warm olive oil in a middling temp. Include diced eggplant, diced zucchini, diced yellow squash, diced red bell pepper, diced onion, and crushed garlic. Cook 'til vegetables are tender, about 8-10 minutes.
3. Include diced tomatoes (with juices), dried thyme, dried basil, salt, and pepper to your skillet. Cook for extra 5 minutes.
4. Spoon the ratatouille mixture into the divided bell peppers, filling them to the top.
5. Drizzle olive oil over the filled bell peppers.
6. Put the filled bell peppers in your air fryer basket.
7. Cook for 25-30 minutes 'til the bell peppers are tender.
8. Present hot.

Per serving: Calories: 222kcal; Fat: 4g; Carbs: 47g; Protein: 8g; Sugar: 23g; Sodium: 38mg; Potassium: 1759mg; Glycemic index: 24

97. Roasted Brussels Sprouts with Balsamic Glaze

Recipe type:
Difficulty: Medium
Preparation time: 15 minutes
Cooking time: 15 minutes
Servings: 2
Ingredients:

- 1/2 lb Brussels sprouts, divided
- 1 tbsp. olive oil
- Salt and pepper as required
- 2 tbsps. balsamic glaze
- Crushed red pepper flakes for garnish (optional)

Directions:

1. In your bowl, toss Brussels sprouts using olive oil, salt, and pepper 'til uniformly covered.
2. Warm up the air fryer to 375 deg.F.
3. Put the seasoned Brussels sprouts in your air fryer basket.
4. Cook for 12-15 minutes, shaking basket halfway through cooking, 'til the Brussels sprouts are crispy and caramelized.
5. Put the roasted Brussels sprouts to your serving dish.
6. Drizzle using balsamic glaze and sprinkle with crushed red pepper flakes if wanted.
7. Present hot.

Per serving: Calories: 118kcal; Fat: 7g; Carbs: 12g; Protein: 4g; Sugar: 5g; Sodium: 31mg; Potassium: 441mg; Glycemic index: 15

98. Zucchini Chips with Herbed Yogurt Dip

Recipe type:
Difficulty: Easy
Preparation time: 15 minutes
Cooking time: 10 minutes
Servings: 2
Ingredients:
Zucchini Chips:

- 2 medium zucchinis, finely cut
- 1 tbsp. olive oil
- 1/4 cup grated Parmesan cheese
- 1/2 tsp. garlic powder
- 1/2 tsp. paprika
- Salt and pepper as required

Herbed Yogurt Dip:

- 1/2 cup Greek yogurt
- 1 tbsp. chopped fresh parsley
- 1 tbsp. chopped fresh dill
- 1 tbsp. chopped fresh chives
- 1 tsp. lemon juice
- Salt and pepper as required

Directions:

1. Warm up the air fryer to 375 deg.F.
2. In your bowl, toss finely cut zucchinis with garlic powder, olive oil, grated Parmesan cheese, paprika, salt, and pepper 'til uniformly covered.
3. Put the seasoned zucchini slices in your air fryer basket in a one layer, ensuring they are not overlapping.
4. Cook for 8-10 minutes, turning them over on the halfway point cooking, 'til the zucchini chips are golden brown and crispy.
5. In another bowl, blend collectively Greek yogurt, chopped fresh parsley, chopped fresh dill, salt, chopped fresh chives, lemon juice, and pepper to make the herbed yogurt dip.
6. Present the zucchini chips hot with the herbed yogurt dip.

Per serving: Calories: 180kcal; Fat: 10g; Carbs: 14g; Protein: 10g; Sugar: 8g; Sodium: 230mg; Potassium: 866mg; Glycemic index: 21

99. Baked Apples with Cinnamon

Recipe type:
Difficulty: Easy
Preparation time: 5 minutes
Cooking time: 15 minutes
Servings: 2
Ingredients:

- 2 apples, cored and divided
- 1 tbsp. melted coconut oil
- 1 tsp. ground cinnamon
- 1 tbsp. maple syrup (optional)

Directions:

1. Warm up the air fryer to 350 deg.F.
2. In your bowl, blend collectively melted coconut oil, ground cinnamon, and maple syrup (if using).
3. Brush the mixture over the cored and divided apples.
4. Put the apples in your air fryer basket, cut-side up.
5. Cook for 12-15 minutes 'til the apples are tender and mildly browned.
6. Present the baked apples hot.

Per serving: Calories: 121kcal; Fat: 7g; Carbs: 18g; Protein: 0.5g; Sugar: 14g; Sodium: 1mg; Potassium: 194mg; Glycemic index: 36

100. Air Fryer Turkey Burgers

Recipe type:
Difficulty: Easy
Preparation time: 10 minutes
Cooking time: 15 minutes
Servings: 2
Ingredients:

- 1/2 lb ground turkey
- 1/4 cup breadcrumbs
- 1 egg
- 1/4 cup finely chopped onion
- 1 clove garlic, crushed
- 1 tsp. Worcestershire sauce
- 1/2 tsp. dried thyme
- Salt and pepper as required
- Burger buns and toppings of choice for presenting

Directions:

1. In your bowl, blend collectively ground turkey, breadcrumbs, egg, finely chopped onion, crushed garlic, Worcestershire sauce, dried thyme, salt, and pepper 'til well blended.
2. Split your mixture into two equal portions then shape each portion into a burger patty.
3. Warm up the air fryer to 375 deg.F.
4. Put the turkey burger patties in your air fryer basket.
5. Cook 12-15 minutes, turning them over on the halfway point cooking, 'til the burgers are cooked through and browned on both sides.
6. Present the turkey burgers on burger buns with toppings of choice.

Per serving: Calories: 245kcal; Fat: 11g; Carbs: 8g; Protein: 27g; Sugar: 1g; Sodium: 231mg; Potassium: 353mg; Glycemic index: 6

101. Crispy Eggplant Parmesan

Recipe type:
Difficulty: Medium
Preparation time: 20 minutes
Cooking time: 15 minutes
Servings: 2
Ingredients:

- 1 big eggplant, cut into rounds
- 1/2 cup breadcrumbs
- 1/4 cup grated Parmesan cheese
- 1 tsp. Italian seasoning
- 1/2 tsp. garlic powder
- 1/2 cup marinara sauce
- 1/2 cup shredded mozzarella cheese
- Fresh basil for garnish (optional)

Directions:

1. Warm up the air fryer to 375 deg.F.
2. In your shallow dish, blend breadcrumbs, grated Parmesan cheese, Italian seasoning, and garlic powder.
3. Dredge eggplant slices in the breadcrumb mixture, pressing to adhere.
4. Put the breaded eggplant slices in your air fryer basket in a one layer.
5. Cook for 10-12 minutes 'til the eggplant is crispy and golden brown.
6. Top each eggplant slice using marinara sauce and shredded mozzarella cheese.
7. Return to the air fryer then cook for extra 3-5 minutes 'til the cheese is melted and bubbly.
8. Garnish using fresh basil and serve hot.

Per serving: Calories: 257kcal; Fat: 10g; Carbs: 32g; Protein: 12g; Sugar: 7g; Sodium: 655mg; Potassium: 712mg; Glycemic index: 28

102. Stuffed Bell Peppers with Quinoa and Black Beans

Recipe type:
Difficulty: Medium
Preparation time: 20 minutes
Cooking time: 20 minutes
Servings: 2
Ingredients:

- 2 big bell peppers, divided and seeds taken out
- 1/2 cup quinoa, washed
- 1 cup vegetable broth
- 1/2 cup cooked black beans
- 1/2 cup corn kernels
- 1/2 cup diced tomatoes
- 1/2 tsp. ground cumin
- 1/2 tsp. chili powder
- Salt and pepper as required
- Fresh cilantro for garnish (optional)
- Lime wedges for presenting (optional)

Directions:

1. In your small saucepan, blend quinoa and vegetable broth. Boil, then decrease temp., cover, then simmer for 15 minutes 'til quinoa is cooked and liquid is immersed.
2. Warm up the air fryer to 375 deg.F.
3. In your bowl, blend collectively cooked quinoa, black beans, corn kernels, diced tomatoes, ground cumin, chili powder, salt, and pepper.
4. Stuff each divided bell pepper with the quinoa and black bean mixture.
5. Put your filled bell peppers in the air fryer basket.
6. Cook for 15-20 minutes 'til the peppers are tender and the filling is heated through.
7. Garnish using fresh cilantro and serve with lime wedges if wanted.

Per serving: Calories: 298kcal; Fat: 2g; Carbs: 60g; Protein: 12g; Sugar: 9g; Sodium: 671mg; Potassium: 1065mg; Glycemic index: 10

28 Days Meal Plan

Day	Breakfast	Snack	Lunch	Snack	Dinner
1	Breakfast Quinoa Bowl with Mixed Fruit (p. 20)	Cottage Cheese with Pineapple Chunks (p. 36)	Lemon Garlic Chicken Skewers (p. 51)	Homemade Granola Bars with Oats, Nuts, and Dried Fruit (p. 33)	Baked Lemon Pepper Mahi Mahi (p. 61)
2	Steel-Cut Oats with Apple Cinnamon Compote (p. 22)	Chia Seed Pudding with Fresh Fruit Topping (p. 33)	Seafood Paella with Shrimp, Mussels, and Clams (p. 57)	Quinoa Salad Jars with Veggies and Lemon Herb Dressing (p. 35)	Pan-Seared Duck Breast with Orange Glaze (p. 53)
3	Fruit Salad with Cottage Cheese (p. 23)	Quinoa Salad Jars with Veggies and Lemon Herb Dressing (p. 35)	Chicken Piccata with Whole Wheat Pasta (p. 52)	Apple Slices with Almond Butter (p. 36)	Grilled Swordfish with Mango Salsa (p. 58)
4	Whole Grain Pancakes with Blueberry Compote (p. 21)	Carrot Sticks with Hummus (p. 35)	Seared Scallops with White Wine Sauce (p. 62)	Cottage Cheese with Pineapple Chunks (p. 36)	Grilled Steak Salad with Balsamic Vinaigrette (p. 52)
5	Greek Yogurt Parfait with Fresh Berries and Almonds (p. 21)	Quinoa Salad Jars with Veggies and Lemon Herb Dressing (p. 35)	Lemon Herb Tilapia (p. 61)	Chia Seed Pudding with Fresh Fruit Topping (p. 33)	Coconut Curry Shrimp with Rice Noodles (p. 60)
6	Steel-Cut Oats with Apple Cinnamon Compote (p. 22)	Quinoa Salad Jars with Veggies and Lemon Herb Dressing (p. 35)	Grilled Steak Salad with Balsamic Vinaigrette (p. 52)	Carrot Sticks with Hummus (p. 35)	Lemon Garlic Chicken Skewers (p. 51)
7	Greek Yogurt Parfait with Fresh Berries and Almonds (p. 21)	Apple Slices with Almond Butter (p. 36)	Baked Tilapia with Tomato and Herb Relish (p. 56)	Banana Chips (p. 36)	Seafood Paella with Shrimp, Mussels, and Clams (p. 57)
8	Whole Grain Pancakes with Blueberry Compote (p. 21)	Apple Slices with Almond Butter (p. 36)	Pan-Seared Sea Bass with Lemon Caper Sauce (p. 59)	Homemade Granola Bars with Oats, Nuts, and Dried Fruit (p. 33)	Pan-Seared Duck Breast with Orange Glaze (p. 53)
9	Whole Grain Pancakes with Blueberry Compote (p. 21)	Vegan Sushi Rolls with Avocado and Cucumber (p. 34)	Grilled Steak Salad with Balsamic Vinaigrette (p. 52)	Seaweed Salad with Sesame Dressing (p. 34)	Seared Scallops with White Wine Sauce (p. 62)

10	Baked Egg Cups with Spinach and Tomato (p. 23)	Vegan Sushi Rolls with Avocado and Cucumber (p. 34)	Broiled Scallops with Garlic Butter (p. 56)	Homemade Granola Bars with Oats, Nuts, and Dried Fruit (p. 33)	Pork Stir-Fry with Snow Peas and Water Chestnuts (p. 54)
11	Baked Egg Cups with Spinach and Tomato (p. 23)	Homemade Granola Bars with Oats, Nuts, and Dried Fruit (p. 33)	Baked Cod with Lemon and Herbs (p. 59)	Homemade Granola Bars with Oats, Nuts, and Dried Fruit (p. 33)	Baked Cod with Lemon and Herbs (p. 59)
12	Egg White Frittata with Spinach, Mushrooms, and Feta (p. 20)	Trail Mix with Nuts, Seeds, and Dried Fruit (p. 34)	Baked Cod with Lemon and Herbs (p. 59)	Vegan Sushi Rolls with Avocado and Cucumber (p. 34)	Turkey Chili with Beans and Corn (p. 51)
13	Oatmeal with Banana and Walnuts (p. 22)	Chia Seed Pudding with Fresh Fruit Topping (p. 33)	Turkey Chili with Beans and Corn (p. 51)	Vegan Sushi Rolls with Avocado and Cucumber (p. 34)	Grilled Lobster with Herb Butter (p. 58)
14	Avocado Toast with Poached Eggs (p. 24)	Seaweed Salad with Sesame Dressing (p. 34)	Grilled Lobster with Herb Butter (p. 58)	Quinoa Salad Jars with Veggies and Lemon Herb Dressing (p. 35)	Pan-Seared Sea Bass with Lemon Caper Sauce (p. 59)
15	Quinoa Breakfast Bowl with Sautéed Vegetables and Egg (p. 24)	Cottage Cheese with Pineapple Chunks (p. 36)	Baked Lemon Pepper Mahi Mahi (p. 61)	Banana Chips (p. 36)	Baked Lemon Pepper Mahi Mahi (p. 61)
16	Breakfast Quinoa Bowl with Mixed Fruit (p. 20)	Chia Seed Pudding with Fresh Fruit Topping (p. 33)	Lemon Herb Tilapia (p. 61)	Vegan Sushi Rolls with Avocado and Cucumber (p. 34)	Pan-Seared Duck Breast with Orange Glaze (p. 53)
17	Fruit Salad with Cottage Cheese (p. 23)	Banana Chips (p. 36)	Chicken Piccata with Whole Wheat Pasta (p. 52)	Trail Mix with Nuts, Seeds, and Dried Fruit (p. 34)	Grilled Swordfish with Mango Salsa (p. 58)
18	Whole Grain Pancakes with Blueberry Compote (p. 21)	Carrot Sticks with Hummus (p. 35)	Seared Scallops with White Wine Sauce (p. 62)	Chia Seed Pudding with Fresh Fruit Topping (p. 33)	Grilled Steak Salad with Balsamic Vinaigrette (p. 52)

19	Greek Yogurt Parfait with Fresh Berries and Almonds (p. 21)	Quinoa Salad Jars with Veggies and Lemon Herb Dressing (p. 35)	Lemon Herb Tilapia (p. 61)	Chia Seed Pudding with Fresh Fruit Topping (p. 33)	Coconut Curry Shrimp with Rice Noodles (p. 60)
20	Steel-Cut Oats with Apple Cinnamon Compote (p. 22)	Quinoa Salad Jars with Veggies and Lemon Herb Dressing (p. 35)	Grilled Steak Salad with Balsamic Vinaigrette (p. 52)	Apple Slices with Almond Butter (p. 36)	Lemon Garlic Chicken Skewers (p. 51)
21	Whole Grain Pancakes with Blueberry Compote (p. 21)	Seaweed Salad with Sesame Dressing (p. 34)	Grilled Steak Salad with Balsamic Vinaigrette (p. 52)	Banana Chips (p. 36)	Seafood Paella with Shrimp, Mussels, and Clams (p. 57)
22	Greek Yogurt Parfait with Fresh Berries and Almonds (p. 21)	Apple Slices with Almond Butter (p. 36)	Pan-Seared Sea Bass with Lemon Caper Sauce (p. 59)	Homemade Granola Bars with Oats, Nuts, and Dried Fruit (p. 33)	Chicken Piccata with Whole Wheat Pasta (p. 52)
23	Whole Grain Pancakes with Blueberry Compote (p. 21)	Apple Slices with Almond Butter (p. 36)	Grilled Steak Salad with Balsamic Vinaigrette (p. 52)	Vegan Sushi Rolls with Avocado and Cucumber (p. 34)	Seared Scallops with White Wine Sauce (p. 62)
24	Fruit Salad with Cottage Cheese (p. 23)	Vegan Sushi Rolls with Avocado and Cucumber (p. 34)	Pan-Seared Duck Breast with Orange Glaze (p. 53)	Trail Mix with Nuts, Seeds, and Dried Fruit (p. 34)	Baked Tilapia with Tomato and Herb Relish (p. 56)
25	Baked Egg Cups with Spinach and Tomato (p. 23)	Homemade Granola Bars with Oats, Nuts, and Dried Fruit (p. 33)	Seared Scallops with White Wine Sauce (p. 62)	Chia Seed Pudding with Fresh Fruit Topping (p. 33)	Pan-Seared Sea Bass with Lemon Caper Sauce (p. 59)
26	Oatmeal with Banana and Walnuts (p. 22)	Chia Seed Pudding with Fresh Fruit Topping (p. 33)	Baked Cod with Lemon and Herbs (p. 59)	Apple Slices with Almond Butter (p. 36)	Turkey Chili with Beans and Corn (p. 51)
27	Avocado Toast with Poached Eggs (p. 24)	Quinoa Salad Jars with Veggies and Lemon Herb Dressing (p. 35)	Turkey Chili with Beans and Corn (p. 51)	Vegan Sushi Rolls with Avocado and Cucumber (p. 34)	Broiled Scallops with Garlic Butter (p. 56)
28	Whole Grain Pancakes with Blueberry Compote (p. 21)	Banana Chips (p. 36)	Grilled Lobster with Herb Butter (p. 58)	Seaweed Salad with Sesame Dressing (p. 34)	Seafood Paella with Shrimp, Mussels, and Clams (p. 57)

Daily List of Ingredients

Day 1:

Produce:
- 1/2 cup quinoa, washed
- 1/2 cup pineapple chunks (fresh or canned in juice)
- 2 pieces garlic
- 1 lemon
- 1/2 tsp. cinnamon
- 1 ripe banana, cut
- 1 cup mixed fresh fruit (e.g., berries, kiwi, mango)
- 2 tbsps. chopped nuts (e.g., almonds, walnuts)
- 1 1/2 cups rolled oats
- 1/4 cup dried fruit (e.g., raisins, cranberries, or apricots)
- 1/4 cup honey or maple syrup
- Wooden skewers
- 1/4 cup almond butter or a peanut butter
- 1 tbsp. coconut oil
- 1/2 tsp. vanilla extract

Dairy:
- 1 cup cottage cheese

Meat and Fish:
- 2 boneless, skinless chicken breasts, cubed
- 2 mahi mahi fillets

Spices and Oils:
- Olive oil (for cooking and dressing)
- Salt and pepper
- Dried oregano
- Dried dill

Optional garnish:
- Fresh parsley
- honey or maple syrup for sweetness

Day 2:

Grains and Legumes:
- 1/2 cup steel-cut oats
- 1 cup paella rice (Arborio or Bomba rice)

Dairy and Alternatives:
- 3 cups water or almond milk

Fruits:
- 2 medium apples
- 1 lemon
- Fresh fruit for topping (e.g., berries, cut bananas, or mango chunks)
- Zest of 1 orange
- 1/2 cup orange juice

Sweeteners and Spices:
- 1 tbsp. maple syrup or honey
- 1 tsp. ground cinnamon
- Pinch of salt
- Salt and pepper as required
- Sea salt as required
- 1 tsp. smoked paprika
- 1/2 tsp. saffron threads
- 2 tbsps. honey
- 1 tbsp. maple syrup (optional)
- 1/2 tsp. vanilla extract

Vegetables:
- 1 onion
- 1 red bell pepper
- 1 tomato
- Fresh parsley for garnish
- Lemon wedges for presenting
- 1 cup cooked quinoa
- 1/4 cup chia seeds
- 1 cup mixed vegetables (e.g., cucumber, bell peppers, cherry tomatoes, carrots)
- 1 tsp. cornstarch (optional, for thickening)

Protein:
- 8 big shrimp

- 8 mussels
- 8 small clams
- 2 duck breast halves
- 2 cups seafood or chicken broth

Herbs and Aromatics:
- 2 pieces garlic
- 2 tbsps. fresh parsley
- 1 tbsp. fresh thyme leaves
- 2 tbsps. lemon herb dressing

Oils:
- 5 tbsp. olive oil

Optional toppings: chopped nuts, raisins, additional maple syrup

Day 3:

Dairy and Substitutes:
- 1 cup cottage cheese

Flavorings:
- 1 tsp. vanilla extract
- 1 tbsp. lemon juice
- 1 tbsp. lime juice

Fruits:
- 1 cup mixed fresh fruits (e.g., strawberries, pineapple, grapes, kiwi)
- 1 apple

Oils and Cooking Fats:
- 2 tbsps. unsalted butter
- 5 tbsp. olive oil

Vegetables and Herbs:
- 2 pieces garlic
- Salt and pepper as required
- 2 tbsps. fresh parsley
- 1/4 cup diced red bell pepper
- 1 ripe mango, skinned and diced
- 2 tbsps. chopped fresh cilantro
- 1 cup mixed vegetables (e.g., cucumber, bell peppers, cherry tomatoes, carrots)
- 1 cup cooked quinoa

Poultry ans Fish:
- 2 swordfish fillets
- 2 boneless, skinless chicken breasts
- 2 halibut fillets

Dry Goods:
- 1/4 cup all-purpose flour (or gluten-free flour)
- Cooked whole wheat pasta, for presenting

Spices:
- 1 jalapeño, sowed and diced

Liquid Ingredients:
- 1/2 cup chicken broth
- 1/4 cup fresh lemon juice

Optional Toppings:
- Shredded coconut
- Mint leaves for garnish
- 2 tbsps. lemon herb dressing
- 1 tbsp. chopped fresh herbs (e.g., parsley, basil, or cilantro)

Additional Ingredients:
- 2 tbsps. almond butter
- 2 tbsps. capers, drained

Day 4:

Fruits and Vegetables:
- 2 carrots, skinned and cut into sticks
- 1/2 cup pineapple chunks (fresh or canned in juice)
- 1/2 cucumber, cut
- 1/4 red onion, finely cut
- 1 cup cherry tomatoes, divided
- 1 cup fresh or frozen blueberries

Dairy and Alternatives:
- 1/4 cup crumbled feta cheese
- 1 cup milk of your choice

- 1 cup cottage cheese

Protein:
- 12 big scallops
- 1/2 lb. lean steak (e.g., sirloin or flank), about 1" dense
- 1 big egg
- 1/4 cup hummus

Pantry Items:
- 1 cup whole wheat flour
- 1 tbsp. baking powder
- Salt and pepper
- 2 tbsps. olive oil
- 1/4 cup dry white wine
- 2 tbsps. unsalted butter
- 1 tbsp. chopped fresh parsley
- Lemon wedges for presenting
- 1 tbsp. Dijon mustard
- 1 tsp. honey
- 1 clove garlic, crushed
- 2 pieces garlic, crushed

Optional Toppings:
- honey or maple syrup for presenting

Salad Ingredients:
- 4 cups mixed salad greens

Salad Dressing Ingredients:
- 2 tbsps. balsamic vinegar
- 1 tbsp. olive oil

Day 5:

Dairy and Fruit:
- 1 cup plain Greek yogurt
- 1/2 cup fresh berries (strawberries, blueberries, raspberries)
- 1/4 cup cut almonds
- 1 cup unsweetened almond milk
- 1 can (13.5 oz) coconut milk
- Fresh fruit for topping (e.g., berries, cut bananas, or mango chunks)

Vegetables and Herbs:
- Fresh parsley for garnish (optional)
- 2 tbsps. lemon herb dressing
- 1 cup mixed vegetables (e.g., cucumber, bell peppers, cherry tomatoes, carrots)
- 1 tbsp. chopped fresh herbs (e.g., parsley, basil, or cilantro)
- 1/4 cup chia seeds
- 1 onion, finely cut
- 1 red bell pepper, finely cut
- 1 carrot, julienned
- 1 zucchini, julienned

Protein:
- 1 tbsp. fish sauce
- 12 big shrimp, skinned and deveined
- 2 tilapia fillets

Grains and Legumes:
- 1 cup cooked quinoa
- 8 oz rice noodles

Condiments and Others:
- Salt and pepper
- 1 tsp. dried thyme
- 4 tbsps. olive oil
- 1 tbsp. lemon juice
- 1 tbsp. honey (optional)
- 1 tbsp. maple syrup (optional)
- Zest and juice of 1 lemon
- 4 pieces garlic, crushed
- 1/2 tsp. vanilla extract
- 1 tbsp. coconut oil
- 1 tbsp. red curry paste
- 1 tbsp. brown sugar
- Juice of 1 lime
- Fresh cilantro for garnish

Day 6:
Dry Goods:
- Wooden skewers
- Salt and pepper
- 1/2 cup steel-cut oats
- 1 tsp. dried oregano
- 2 tsp. ground cinnamon

Sweeteners:
- 4 tbsp. honey or maple syrup

Dairy/Alternatives:
- 4 cup almond milk
- 1/4 cup crumbled feta cheese

Fruits and Vegetables:
- 4 medium apples
- 2 carrots
- Fresh parsley leaves
- 1/2 cup steel-cut oats
- 4 cups mixed salad greens
- 1 cup cherry tomatoes, divided
- 1/2 cucumber, cut
- 1/4 red onion, finely cut

Meat, Fish and Poultry:
- 1/2 lb. lean steak (e.g., sirloin or flank), about 1" dense
- 2 boneless, skinless chicken breasts, cubes

Condiments:
- Olive oil
- 1 lemon, juiced and zested
- Hummus
- 2 tbsps. balsamic vinegar

Spices and Herbs:
- 1 clove garlic
- 2 pieces garlic, crushed
- 1 tsp. Dijon mustard

Optionals:
- chopped nuts, raisins, additional maple syrup

Day 7:
Produce:
- 1 diced bell pepper
- 1 diced tomato
- 2 tbsps. fresh parsley, chopped
- 1 apple, cored then cut
- 2 tomatoes
- 2 ripe bananas
- 1/4 cup cut almonds
- 1/2 cup fresh berries (e.g., strawberries, blueberries, raspberries)
- 1 tbsp. honey (optional)
- 1 cup paella rice (Arborio or Bomba rice)

Condiments and Disperses:
- Salt and Pepper
- 2 tbsps. almond butter
- Lemon wedges for presenting
- 1 tsp. smoked paprika
- 1/2 tsp. saffron threads

Dairy:
- 1 cup plain Greek yogurt

Fish and Poultry:
- 4 big eggs
- 2 tilapia fillets
- 2 cups seafood or chicken broth
- 8 big shrimp, skinned and deveined
- 8 mussels, cleaned and debearded
- 8 small clams, scrubbed

Herbs and Seasonings:
- 1 tbsps. fresh parsley, chopped
- 4 pieces garlic, crushed
- 1 onion, chopped

Oils:
- 3 tbsps. olive oil

Day 8:

Bakery & Baking
- Whole wheat flour (1 cup)
- Baking powder (1 tbsp)
- Rolled oats (1 1/2 cups)

Dairy & Eggs
- Milk of your choice (1 cup)
- Egg (1 big)
- Unsalted butter (2 tbsps)

Meat & Seafood
- Sea bass fillets (2)
- Duck breast halves (2)

Fruits & Vegetables
- Blueberries (1 cup fresh or frozen)
- Apple (1, cored then cut)
- Lemon (1, zest and juice)
- Garlic (4 pieces, crushed)
- Fresh parsley (for garnish)
- Orange (1, zest and 1/2 cup juice)

Condiments & Spices
- Honey or maple syrup (1/4 cup + 1 tbsp + optional additional for presenting)
- Almond butter or peanut butter (2 tbsps + 1/4 cup)
- Olive oil (3 tbsps)
- Capers (2 tbsps, drained)
- Coconut oil (1 tbsp)
- Vanilla extract (1/2 tsp)
- Salt
- Pepper
- Fresh thyme leaves (1 tsp)
- Cornstarch (1 tsp, optional for thickening)

Nuts & Dried Fruits
- Chopped nuts (1/2 cup, e.g., almonds, walnuts, or pecans)
- Dried fruit (1/4 cup, e.g., raisins, cranberries, or apricots, chopped)

Day 9:

Bakery & Baking
- Whole wheat flour: 1 cup
- Baking powder: 1 tbsp
- Honey or maple syrup: 1 tbsp + optional for presenting
- Sushi rice (cooked): 1 cup

Dairy & Eggs
- Milk of your choice: 1 cup
- Egg: 1 big

Seafood
- Nori seaweed sheets: 2 sheets
- Scallops: 12 large

Meat
- Lean steak (e.g., sirloin or flank): 1/2 lb (about 1" thick)

Fruits & Vegetables
- Blueberries: 1 cup fresh or frozen
- Avocado: 1/2
- Cucumber: 1/2 (julienned) + 1/2 (cut)
- Cherry tomatoes: 1 cup (divided)
- Red onion: 1/4 (finely sliced)
- Mixed salad greens: 4 cups
- Garlic: 3 cloves (crushed)

Condiments & Spices
- Soy sauce
- Wasabi (optional)
- Pickled ginger (optional)
- Salt
- Pepper
- Balsamic vinegar: 2 tbsps
- Olive oil: 2 tbsps + 1 tbsp
- Dijon mustard: 1 tsp
- Rice vinegar: 2 tbsps
- Sesame oil: 1 tbsp
- Grated ginger: 1 tsp
- Sesame seeds: 1 tsp

- Chili flakes (optional): 1/2 tsp

Cheese
- Feta cheese: 1/4 cup (crumbled)

Fresh Herbs
- Fresh parsley: 1 tbsp (chopped)
- Green onion (optional): 1 (finely sliced)

Other
- Mixed seaweed salad (e.g., wakame, hijiki, or kombu): 2 cups
- Dry white wine: 1/4 cup
- Unsalted butter: 2 tbsps
- Lemon wedges (for serving)
- Salad Dressing Ingredients
- Honey: 1 tsp
- Garlic: 1 clove (crushed)

Day 10:

Dairy & Eggs
- Eggs: 4 large
- Shredded cheese (any variety): 1/4 cup

Produce
- Fresh spinach leaves: 1 cup (chopped)
- Tomatoes: 1/2 cup (diced)
- Avocado: 1/2
- Cucumber: 1/2 (julienned)
- Garlic: 4 cloves (2 crushed for scallops, 2 crushed for pork dish)
- Fresh parsley (optional): for garnish

Seafood
- Nori seaweed sheets: 2 sheets
- Scallops: 8 large

Grains & Cereals
- Rolled oats: 1 1/2 cups
- Cooked sushi rice: 1 cup

Nuts & Dried Fruits
- Chopped nuts (e.g., almonds, walnuts, or pecans): 1/2 cup
- Dried fruit (e.g., raisins, cranberries, or apricots): 1/4 cup (chopped)

Condiments & Sauces
- Soy sauce: 2 tbsps
- Wasabi (optional)
- Pickled ginger (optional)
- Almond butter or peanut butter: 1/4 cup
- Honey or maple syrup: 1/4 cup + 1 tbsp
- Olive oil: for cooking + 1 tbsp

Baking & Cooking
- Coconut oil: 1 tbsp
- Vanilla extract: 1/2 tsp

Meat
- Pork tenderloin: 1/2 lb (finely cut)

Canned Goods
- Water chestnuts: 1 can (8 oz), drained and cut

Other
- Lemon juice: 1 tbsp
- Lemon wedges: for serving
- Cooked rice: for serving

Day 11:

Dairy & Eggs
- Eggs: 4 large

Produce
- Fresh spinach leaves: 1 cup (chopped)
- Tomatoes: 1/2 cup (diced)
- Lemon: 2 (1 for cod dish, 1 for oats)

Cheese & Nuts
- Shredded cheese (any variety): 1/4 cup
- Chopped nuts (e.g., almonds, walnuts, or pecans): 1/2 cup

Grains & Cereals

- Rolled oats: 3 cups (1 1/2 cups for oats recipe, 1 1/2 cups for another oats recipe)
- Dried fruit (e.g., raisins, cranberries, or apricots): 1/2 cup (1/4 cup for each oats recipe)

Condiments & Spices

- Honey or maple syrup: 1/2 cup (1/4 cup for each oats recipe)
- Almond butter or peanut butter: 1/2 cup (1/4 cup for each oats recipe)
- Coconut oil: 2 tbsps (1 tbsp for each oats recipe)
- Vanilla extract: 1 tsp (1/2 tsp for each oats recipe)
- Salt
- Pepper
- Olive oil: 4 tbsps (2 tbsps for each cod dish)

Herbs & Spices

- Garlic: 4 cloves (2 for each cod dish)
- Dried thyme: 2 tsp (1 tsp for each cod dish)

Meat & Seafood

- Cod fillets: 4 pieces

Day 12:

Dairy & Eggs

- Egg whites: 6
- Crumbled feta cheese: 1/4 cup

Produce

- Spinach leaves: 1 cup (chopped)
- Mushrooms: 1/2 cup (cut)
- Avocado: 1 (cut into halves)
- Cucumber: 1 (julienned)
- Lemon: 1 (cut)
- Garlic: 4 cloves (crushed)
- Onion: 1 small (diced)
- Bell pepper: 1 (diced)
- Corn kernels: 1 cup (fresh or frozen)

Meat & Seafood

- Cod fillets: 2
- Ground turkey: 1/2 lb

Canned Goods

- Diced tomatoes: 1 can (14.5 oz)
- Kidney beans: 1 can (15 oz)

Grains & Cereals

- Cooked sushi rice: 2 cups

Condiments & Spices

- Olive oil: 3 tbsps + extra for cooking
- Dried thyme: 1 tsp
- Chili powder: 1 tbsp
- Ground cumin: 1 tsp
- Salt
- Pepper
- Soy sauce (optional for presenting)
- Wasabi (optional for presenting)
- Pickled ginger (optional for presenting)

Seaweed

- Nori seaweed sheets: 4 sheets

Day 13:

Dairy & Eggs

- Milk: 2 cups (if not using water)
- Unsalted butter: 4 tbsps (melted)

Produce

- Banana: 1 (ripe, cut)
- Chopped walnuts: 1/4 cup + 1/2 cup = 3/4 cup
- Dried fruit (e.g., raisins, cranberries, or apricots), chopped: 1/4 cup
- Small onion: 1 (diced)
- Bell pepper: 1 (diced)
- Garlic: 4 cloves (crushed)
- Fresh parsley: 1 tbsp (chopped)
- Fresh thyme: 1 tbsp (chopped)
- Lemon: 1 (cut into wedges)

- Avocado: 1/2
- Cucumber: 1/2 (julienned)
- Corn kernels: 1 cup (fresh or frozen)

Grains & Cereals
- Old-fashioned oats: 1 cup
- Rolled oats: 1 1/2 cups
- Nori seaweed sheets: 2 sheets
- Cooked sushi rice: 1 cup

Meat & Seafood
- Ground turkey: 1/2 lb
- Whole lobsters: 2 (split in half lengthwise)

Canned Goods
- Diced tomatoes: 1 can (14.5 oz)
- Kidney beans: 1 can (15 oz)

Condiments & Spices
- Honey or maple syrup: 1/4 cup + optional for sweetness
- Almond butter or peanut butter: 1/4 cup
- Coconut oil: 1 tbsp
- Vanilla extract: 1/2 tsp
- Chili powder: 1 tbsp
- Ground cumin: 1 tsp
- Salt
- Pepper
- Olive oil: 1 tbsp + extra for cooking
- Soy sauce (optional for presenting)
- Wasabi (optional for presenting)
- Pickled ginger (optional for presenting)

Day 14:
Bakery
- Whole wheat bread: 2 slices

Dairy & Eggs
- Big eggs: 2
- Unsalted butter: 6 tbsps (melted)
- Olive oil: 4 tbsps

Produce
- Ripe avocado: 1
- Garlic: 4 cloves (crushed)
- Fresh parsley: 2 tbsps (chopped) + extra for garnish
- Fresh thyme: 1 tbsp (chopped)
- Lemon: 1 (for zest and juice) + lemon wedges for presenting
- Green onion: 1 (finely cut, optional)
- Mixed vegetables (e.g., cucumber, bell peppers, cherry tomatoes, carrots): 1 cup

Seafood
- Whole lobsters: 2 (split in half lengthwise)
- Sea bass fillets: 2
- Mixed seaweed salad (e.g., wakame, hijiki, or kombu): 2 cups

Grains & Cereals
- Cooked quinoa: 1 cup

Condiments & Spices
- Rice vinegar: 2 tbsps
- Soy sauce: 1 tbsp
- Sesame oil: 1 tbsp
- Honey or maple syrup: 1 tsp
- Grated ginger: 1 tsp
- Sesame seeds: 1 tsp
- Chili flakes: 1/2 tsp (optional)
- Capers: 2 tbsps (drained)
- Salt
- Pepper
- Lemon herb dressing: 2 tbsps

Herbs
- Fresh herbs (e.g., parsley, basil, or cilantro): 1 tbsp (chopped)

Day 15:
Grains & Cereals
- Quinoa: 1/2 cup

Dairy & Eggs

- Big eggs: 2
- Cottage cheese: 1 cup

Produce

- Bell peppers: 1/2 cup (diced)
- Zucchini: 1/2 cup (diced)
- Onion: 1/4 cup (diced)
- Garlic: 2 cloves (crushed)
- Parsley: Optional for garnish
- Pineapple chunks (fresh or canned in juice): 1/2 cup
- Bananas: 2
- Lemon: 1 (for zest and juice)

Seafood

- Mahi mahi fillets: 4

Condiments & Spices

- Olive oil: 3 tbsps
- Black pepper: 2 tsps
- Salt: as required
- Broth

- Water or vegetable broth: 1 cup

Day 16:

Grains & Cereals

- Quinoa: 1/2 cup
- Rolled oats: 1 1/2 cups
- Nori seaweed sheets: 2
- Sushi rice: 1 cup (cooked)

Dairy & Alternatives

- Milk: 1 cup (or water)
- Almond butter or peanut butter: 1/4 cup

Produce

- Banana: 1 (ripe, cut)
- Mixed fresh fruit: 1/2 cup (e.g., berries, kiwi, mango)
- Lemon: 1 (for zest and juice)
- Orange: 1 (for zest and juice)
- Garlic: 4 cloves (crushed)
- Avocado: 1/2 (cut)
- Cucumber: 1/2 (julienned)
- Fresh parsley: Optional for garnish
- Fresh thyme leaves: 1 tsp

Meat & Seafood

- Tilapia fillets: 2
- Duck breast halves: 2

Nuts & Seeds

- Chopped nuts (e.g., almonds, walnuts, or pecans): 1/2 cup + 2 tbsps
- Dried fruit (e.g., raisins, cranberries, or apricots): 1/4 cup

Condiments & Spices

- Olive oil: 3 tbsps
- Coconut oil: 1 tbsp
- Honey or maple syrup: 1/4 cup + 2 tbsps
- Vanilla extract: 1/2 tsp
- Cinnamon: 1/2 tsp
- Dried thyme: 1 tsp
- Salt and pepper: as required
- Cornstarch: 1 tsp (optional)
- Soy sauce: for presenting (optional)
- Wasabi: for presenting (optional)
- Pickled ginger: for presenting (optional)

Liquids

- Orange juice: 1/2 cup

Day 17:

Dairy & Alternatives

- Cottage cheese: 1 cup

Produce

- Mixed fresh fruits (e.g., strawberries, pineapple, grapes, kiwi): 1 cup
- Mint leaves: Optional for garnish
- Bananas: 4 (ripe)

- Garlic: 2 cloves (crushed)
- Lemon: 1 (for fresh lemon juice)
- Avocado: 1/2 (cut)
- Cucumber: 1/2 (julienned)
- Mango: 1 (ripe, skinned, and diced)
- Red onion: 1/4 cup (diced)
- Red bell pepper: 1/4 cup (diced)
- Jalapeño: 1 (sowed and diced)
- Fresh parsley: 2 tbsps (chopped)
- Fresh cilantro: 2 tbsps (chopped)
- Lime: 1 (for juice)

Meat & Seafood
- Boneless, skinless chicken breasts: 2 (pounded)
- Swordfish fillets: 2

Nuts & Seeds
- Almonds: 1/4 cup
- Cashews: 1/4 cup
- Pumpkin seeds: 2 tbsps
- Sunflower seeds: 2 tbsps

Grains & Cereals
- Nori seaweed sheets: 2
- Sushi rice: 1 cup (cooked)
- All-purpose flour (gluten-free): 1/4 cup
- Whole wheat pasta: for presenting

Condiments & Spices
- Olive oil: 3 tbsps
- Unsalted butter: 2 tbsps
- Capers: 2 tbsps (drained)
- Soy sauce: for presenting (optional)
- Wasabi: for presenting (optional)
- Pickled ginger: for presenting (optional)
- Dried cranberries: 2 tbsps
- Raisins: 2 tbsps
- Salt and pepper: as required

Liquids
- Chicken broth: 1/2 cup
- Lime juice: 1 tbsp

Day 18:

Bakery & Baking
- Whole wheat flour: 1 cup
- Baking powder: 1 tbsp
- Honey or maple syrup: 2 tbsp + additional for presenting (optional)
- Dijon mustard: 1 tsp

Dairy & Alternatives
- Milk of your choice: 1 cup
- Unsweetened almond milk: 1 cup
- Big egg: 1
- Unsalted butter: 2 tbsps
- Crumbled feta cheese: 1/4 cup

Produce
- Fresh or frozen blueberries: 1 cup
- Carrots: 2 (skinned and cut into sticks)
- Garlic: 3 cloves (crushed)
- Fresh parsley: 1 tbsp (chopped)
- Lemon: wedges for presenting
- Fresh fruit for topping (e.g., berries, cut bananas, or mango chunks): as desired
- Mixed salad greens: 4 cups
- Cherry tomatoes: 1 cup
- Cucumber: 1/2 (cut)
- Red onion: 1/4 (finely cut)

Meat & Seafood
- Big scallops: 12
- Lean steak (e.g., sirloin or flank), about 1" dense: 1/2 lb
- Canned & Packaged

- Hummus: 1/4 cup
- Chia seeds: 1/4 cup

Condiments & Spices

- Salt and pepper: as required
- Olive oil: 5 tbsps
- Dry white wine: 1/4 cup
- Balsamic vinegar: 2 tbsps
- Maple syrup: 1 tbsp (optional)
- Vanilla extract: 1/2 tsp

Additional

- Lemon wedges for presenting

Day 19:

Dairy & Alternatives

- Plain Greek yogurt: 1 cup
- Unsweetened almond milk: 1 cup

Fruits

- Fresh berries (e.g., strawberries, blueberries, raspberries): 1/2 cup + additional for topping
- Fresh fruit for topping (e.g., berries, cut bananas, or mango chunks): as desired
- Lemon: 1
- Lime: 1

Vegetables

- Mixed vegetables (e.g., cucumber, bell peppers, cherry tomatoes, carrots): 1 cup
- Onion: 1 (finely cut)
- Red bell pepper: 1 (finely cut)
- Carrot: 1 (julienned)
- Zucchini: 1 (julienned)
- Fresh herbs (e.g., parsley, basil, or cilantro): 1 tbsp + fresh parsley for garnish (optional)
- Garlic: 4 cloves (crushed)

Meat & Seafood

- Tilapia fillets: 2
- Big shrimp, skinned and deveined: 12

Canned & Packaged Goods

- Quinoa, cooked: 1 cup
- Rice noodles: 8 oz
- Coconut milk (13.5 oz): 1 can

Condiments & Spices

- Honey: 1 tbsp (optional)
- Lemon herb dressing: 2 tbsps
- Olive oil: 4 tbsps
- Lemon juice: 1 tbsp
- Maple syrup: 1 tbsp (optional)
- Vanilla extract: 1/2 tsp
- Dried thyme: 1 tsp
- Red curry paste: 1 tbsp
- Fish sauce: 1 tbsp
- Brown sugar: 1 tbsp
- Salt and pepper: as required

Nuts & Seeds

- Cut almonds: 1/4 cup
- Chia seeds: 1/4 cup

Oils & Fats

- Coconut oil: 1 tbsp

Day 20:

Grains & Legumes

- Steel-cut oats: 1/2 cup
- Quinoa, cooked: 1 cup

Dairy & Alternatives

- Almond milk: 2 cups
- Crumbled feta cheese: 1/4 cup

Fruits

- Apples: 3 (2 medium, 1 for cutting)
- Lemon: 1 (juiced and zested)

Vegetables

- Mixed vegetables (e.g., cucumber, bell peppers, cherry tomatoes, carrots): 1 cup
- Cherry tomatoes: 1 cup
- Cucumber: 1/2 (cut)
- Red onion: 1/4 (finely cut)

- Mixed salad greens: 4 cups

Meat & Seafood

- Lean steak (e.g., sirloin or flank), about 1" dense: 1/2 lb
- Boneless, skinless chicken breasts, cubes: 2

Condiments & Spices

- Maple syrup or honey: 1 tbsp (for oats) + 1 tsp (for dressing) + optional additional for topping
- Ground cinnamon: 1 tsp
- Salt and pepper: as required
- Lemon herb dressing: 2 tbsps
- Olive oil: 6 tbsps (2 for quinoa salad, 1 for salad dressing, 2 for chicken, 1 for steak)
- Lemon juice: 1 tbsp + juice of 1 lemon
- Chopped fresh herbs (e.g., parsley, basil, or cilantro): 1 tbsp
- Balsamic vinegar: 2 tbsps
- Dijon mustard: 1 tsp
- Dried oregano: 1 tsp
- Garlic: 3 cloves (crushed)
- Pinch of salt

Nuts & Seeds

- Chopped nuts (optional for topping)
- Raisins (optional for topping)
- Almond butter: 2 tbsps

Others

- Wooden skewers, soaked in water for 30 minutes

Day 21:

Grains & Baking

- Whole wheat flour: 1 cup
- Baking powder: 1 tbsp
- Paella rice (Arborio or Bomba rice): 1 cup

Dairy & Alternatives

- Milk of your choice: 1 cup
- Big egg: 1
- Crumbled feta cheese: 1/4 cup

Fruits

- Fresh or frozen blueberries: 1 cup
- Ripe bananas: 2
- Lemon wedges for presenting: 1 lemon

Vegetables

- Green onion (optional): 1 (finely cut)
- Cucumber: 1/2 (cut)
- Red onion: 1/4 (finely cut)
- Mixed salad greens: 4 cups
- Cherry tomatoes: 1 cup (divided)
- Onion: 1 (chopped)
- Red bell pepper: 1 (diced)
- Tomato: 1 (diced)
- Fresh parsley for garnish

Meat & Seafood

- Lean steak (e.g., sirloin or flank), about 1" dense: 1/2 lb
- Big shrimp, skinned and deveined: 8
- Mussels, cleaned and debearded: 8
- Small clams, scrubbed: 8

Condiments & Spices

- Honey or maple syrup: 1 tbsp + 1 tsp (for recipes) + optional additional for presenting
- Soy sauce: 1 tbsp
- Sesame oil: 1 tbsp
- Grated ginger: 1 tsp
- Sesame seeds: 1 tsp
- Chili flakes (optional): 1/2 tsp
- Balsamic vinegar: 2 tbsps
- Olive oil: 3 tbsps (1 for salad, 2 for paella)
- Dijon mustard: 1 tsp
- Garlic: 3 cloves (crushed)
- Rice vinegar: 2 tbsps
- Smoked paprika: 1 tsp

- Saffron threads: 1/2 tsp
- Salt and pepper as required

Seafood

- Mixed seaweed salad (e.g., wakame, hijiki, or kombu): 2 cups
- Seafood or chicken broth: 2 cups

Day 22:

Dairy & Alternatives

- Plain Greek yogurt: 1 cup
- Unsalted butter: 4 tbsps (2 for sea bass, 2 for chicken)
- Almond butter: 4 tbsps (2 for apple, 2 for recipe)
- Plain Greek yogurt: 1 cup

Fruits

- Fresh berries (e.g., strawberries, blueberries, raspberries): 1/2 cup
- Apple: 1
- Lemon: 1 (zest and juice)
- Dried fruit (e.g., raisins, cranberries, or apricots), chopped: 1/4 cup

Vegetables & Herbs

- Garlic: 4 cloves (crushed)
- Fresh parsley, chopped: 2 tbsps + garnish

Meat & Seafood

- Sea bass fillets: 2
- Boneless, skinless chicken breasts, pounded: 2

Nuts & Seeds

- Cut almonds: 1/4 cup
- Chopped nuts (e.g., almonds, walnuts, or pecans): 1/2 cup

Grains & Baking

- Rolled oats: 1 1/2 cups
- All-purpose flour (gluten-free flour): 1/4 cup

Condiments & Spices

- Honey (optional): 1 tbsp + 1/4 cup
- Olive oil: 4 tbsps (2 for sea bass, 2 for chicken)
- Coconut oil: 1 tbsp
- Vanilla extract: 1/2 tsp
- Salt and pepper: as required
- Capers, drained: 4 tbsps (2 for sea bass, 2 for chicken)
- Chicken broth: 1/2 cup
- Fresh lemon juice: 1/4 cup

Pasta

- Cooked whole wheat pasta: for presenting

Day 23:

Dairy & Alternatives

- Milk of your choice: 1 cup
- Unsalted butter: 2 tbsps
- Crumbled feta cheese: 1/4 cup

Fruits

- Fresh or frozen blueberries: 1 cup
- Apple: 1
- Lemon wedges: for presenting
- Avocado: 1/2 (cut)

Vegetables & Herbs

- Mixed salad greens: 4 cups
- Cherry tomatoes: 1 cup
- Cucumber: 1 (1/2 cut, 1/2 julienned)
- Red onion: 1/4 (finely cut)
- Fresh parsley: 1 tbsp (chopped)
- Garlic: 3 cloves (crushed)

Meat & Seafood

- Lean steak (e.g., sirloin or flank): 1/2 lb
- Scallops: 12 big

Pantry Items

- Whole wheat flour: 1 cup

- Baking powder: 1 tbsp
- Honey or maple syrup: 1 tbsp + additional for presenting (optional)
- Olive oil: 3 tbsps
- Balsamic vinegar: 2 tbsps
- Dijon mustard: 1 tsp
- Almond butter: 2 tbsps
- Dry white wine: 1/4 cup
- Nori seaweed sheets: 2
- Cooked sushi rice: 1 cup
- Soy sauce: for presenting (optional)
- Wasabi: for presenting (optional)
- Pickled ginger: for presenting (optional)
- Sushi rice: 1 cup (cooked)
- Salt and pepper: as required

Eggs
- Big egg: 1

Condiments & Spices
- Salt and pepper: as required

Day 24:
Dairy & Alternatives
- Cottage cheese: 1 cup

Fruits
- Mixed fresh fruits: 1 cup
- Avocado: 1/2
- Orange: 1
- Lemon wedges: for presenting

Vegetables & Herbs
- Cucumber: 1/2
- Garlic: 4 cloves
- Fresh thyme leaves: 1 tsp
- Fresh parsley: 2 tbsps
- Fresh basil: 1 tbsp
- Tomatoes: 2
- Mint leaves: optional

Meat & Seafood
- Duck breast halves: 2
- Tilapia fillets: 2

Pantry Items
- Nori seaweed sheets: 2
- Cooked sushi rice: 1 cup
- Soy sauce: optional
- Wasabi: optional
- Pickled ginger: optional
- Orange juice: 1/2 cup
- Honey: 2 tbsps
- Cornstarch: 1 tsp (optional)
- Almonds: 1/4 cup
- Cashews: 1/4 cup
- Pumpkin seeds: 2 tbsps
- Sunflower seeds: 2 tbsps
- Dried cranberries: 2 tbsps
- Raisins: 2 tbsps
- Olive oil: 3 tbsps
- Salt and pepper: as required

Day 25:
Dairy & Alternatives
- Eggs: 4
- Shredded cheese: 1/4 cup
- Unsweetened almond milk: 1 cup

Vegetables & Herbs
- Spinach leaves: 1 cup (chopped)
- Tomatoes: 1/2 cup (diced)
- Fresh parsley: 1 tbsp (chopped) + for garnish
- Garlic: 4 cloves (crushed)
- Lemon: 1 (zest and juice) + wedges for presenting

Fruits
- Fresh fruit for topping (e.g., berries, cut bananas, or mango chunks)
- Seafood

- Scallops: 12
- Sea bass fillets: 2

Pantry Items

- Olive oil or cooking spray
- Olive oil: 4 tbsps
- Unsalted butter: 4 tbsps
- Dry white wine: 1/4 cup
- Rolled oats: 1 1/2 cups
- Chopped nuts: 1/2 cup
- Dried fruit: 1/4 cup (chopped)
- Honey or maple syrup: 1/4 cup + 1 tbsp (optional)
- Almond butter or peanut butter: 1/4 cup
- Coconut oil: 1 tbsp
- Vanilla extract: 1 tsp
- Chia seeds: 1/4 cup
- Capers: 2 tbsps (drained)
- Salt and pepper: as required

Day 26:

Dairy & Alternatives

- Milk or unsweetened almond milk: 2 cups + 1 cup
- Honey or maple syrup: 1 tbsp (optional)
- Vanilla extract: 1/2 tsp

Fruits

- Ripe banana: 1
- Fresh fruit for topping
- Apple: 1
- Lemon: 1 (cut)

Vegetables

- Small onion: 1 (diced)
- Bell pepper: 1 (diced)
- Corn kernels: 1 cup
- Garlic: 4 pieces (crushed)

Protein

- Cod fillets: 2
- Ground turkey: 1/2 lb

Canned Goods

- Diced tomatoes (14.5 oz): 1 can
- Kidney beans (15 oz): 1 can

Grains & Nuts

- Old-fashioned oats: 1 cup
- Chia seeds: 1/4 cup
- Chopped walnuts: 1/4 cup

Spices & Seasonings

- Dried thyme: 1 tsp
- Chili powder: 1 tbsp
- Ground cumin: 1 tsp
- Salt and pepper: as required

Condiments & Cooking

- Olive oil: 2 tbsps + for cooking
- Almond butter: 2 tbsps

Day 27:

Bakery & Grains

- Whole wheat bread: 2 slices
- Cooked quinoa: 1 cup
- Cooked sushi rice: 1 cup

Dairy & Eggs

- Big eggs: 2
- Unsalted butter: 2 tbsps, melted

Meat & Seafood

- Ground turkey: 1/2 lb
- Big scallops: 8

Vegetables

- Ripe avocado: 1 + 1/2 (cut)
- Mixed vegetables: 1 cup
- Small onion: 1 (diced)
- Bell pepper: 1 (diced)
- Cucumber: 1/2 (julienned)
- Garlic: 4 pieces (crushed)
- Lemon wedges for presenting

- Canned & Jarred Goods

- Diced tomatoes (14.5 oz): 1 can
- Kidney beans (15 oz): 1 can

Condiments & Sauces

- Lemon herb dressing: 2 tbsps
- Olive oil: 2 tbsps + for cooking
- Lemon juice: 2 tbsps
- Soy sauce and wasabi for presenting (optional)
- Pickled ginger for presenting (optional)

Herbs & Spices

- Chopped fresh herbs: 1 tbsp
- Chili powder: 1 tbsp
- Ground cumin: 1 tsp
- Salt and pepper: as required
- Chopped fresh parsley for garnish (optional)

Other

- Nori seaweed sheets: 2

Day 28:

Bakery & Grains

- Whole wheat flour: 1 cup
- Paella rice: 1 cup

Dairy & Eggs

- Milk: 1 cup
- Egg: 1
- Unsalted butter: 4 tbsps, melted

Meat & Seafood

- Whole lobsters: 2
- Big shrimp: 8
- Mussels: 8
- Small clams: 8

Vegetables & Herbs

- Blueberries: 1 cup
- Bananas: 2
- Garlic: 4 pieces
- Parsley: 1 tbsp + for garnish
- Thyme: 1 tbsp
- Lemon wedges
- Mixed seaweed salad: 2 cups
- Ginger: 1 tsp
- Green onion: 1 (optional)
- Onion: 1
- Red bell pepper: 1
- Tomato: 1

Canned & Jarred Goods

- Seafood or chicken broth: 2 cups

Condiments & Sauces

- Honey or maple syrup: 1 tbsp + optional for presenting
- Rice vinegar: 2 tbsps
- Soy sauce: 1 tbsp
- Sesame oil: 1 tbsp
- Sesame seeds: 1 tsp
- Olive oil: 2 tbsps

Herbs & Spices

- Baking powder: 1 tbsp
- Salt and pepper
- Chili flakes: 1/2 tsp (optional)
- Smoked paprika: 1 tsp
- Saffron threads: 1/2 tsp

Conversion Chart

Volume Equivalents (Liquid)		
US Standard	US Standard (oz.)	Metric (approximate)
2 tbsps.	1 fl. oz.	30 milliliter
¼ cup	2 fl. oz.	60 milliliter
½ cup	4 fl. oz.	120 milliliter
1 cup	8 fl. oz.	240 milliliter
1½ cups	12 fl. oz.	355 milliliter
2 cups or 1 pint	16 fl. oz.	475 milliliter
4 cups or 1 quart	32 fl. oz.	1 Liter
1 gallon	128 fl. oz.	4 Liter

Volume Equivalents (Dry)	
US Standard	Metric (approximate)
⅛ tsp.	0.5 milliliter
¼ tsp.	1 milliliter
½ tsp.	2 milliliter
¾ tsp.	4 milliliter
1 tsp.	5 milliliter
1 tbsp.	15 milliliter
¼ cup	59 milliliter
⅓ cup	79 milliliter
½ cup	118 milliliter
⅔ cup	156 milliliter
¾ cup	177 milliliter
1 cup	235 milliliter
2 cups or 1 pint	475 milliliter
3 cups	700 milliliter
4 cups or 1 quart	1 Liter

Oven Temperatures	
Fahrenheit (F)	Celsius (C) (approximate)
250 deg.F	120 deg.C
300 deg.F	150 deg.C
325 deg.F	165 deg.C
350 deg.F	180 deg.C
375 deg.F	190 deg.C
400 deg.F	200 deg.C
425 deg.F	220 deg.C
450 deg.F	230 deg.C

Weight Equivalents	
US Standard	Metric (approximate)
1 tbsp.	15 g
½ oz.	15 g
1 oz.	30 g
2 oz.	60 g
4 oz.	115 g
8 oz.	225 g
12 oz.	340 g
16 oz. or 1 lb.	455 g

Conclusion

When it comes to managing your cholesterol levels, it's essential to engage in open communication with your healthcare provider. Together, you can devise a tailored plan that suits your individual needs and addresses any underlying medical conditions. Lifestyle adjustments such as reducing saturated fat intake can be effective for some individuals, while others may require a combination of lifestyle changes and medication.

Your healthcare provider will consider various factors including your medical history, family history, and lifestyle habits to formulate a comprehensive approach to lowering your cholesterol. It's crucial to understand that achieving optimal cholesterol levels may take time, and setbacks can occur along the way. Don't hesitate to communicate any challenges or concerns you encounter during your journey.

Despite your best efforts, it's important to recognize that factors beyond your control, such as the body's natural cholesterol production by the liver, can influence cholesterol levels. Managing cholesterol is a multifaceted process that involves both proactive lifestyle modifications and potentially medical interventions.

Remember, having high cholesterol isn't a reflection of personal failure but rather a complex interplay of physiological processes. Embrace the journey one step at a time, and remain proactive in taking charge of your health. Should lifestyle changes alone not yield the desired results, medications and other medical interventions can complement your efforts to optimize your cholesterol levels and overall well-being.

And as you delve into managing your health, why not explore the delightful recipes within this book? Nourishing your body with wholesome, cholesterol-friendly meals can be both satisfying and beneficial for your overall health journey. So, expand your culinary horizons and try out the recipes provided—they may just become an integral part of your cholesterol management plan.

Bonus

Download your bonus ebook "Healthy Italian Recipes"

Direct link: https://drive.google.com/file/d/192kUuGcKsU3qwi5TYEeQNAz8ZqR4h63y/view?usp=sharing

 Or scan this QR Code with your smartphone or tablet

Index

Air Fryer Turkey Burgers; 86
Air Fryer Veggie Tacos; 83
Apple Slices with Almond Butter; 37
Asparagus Risotto with Parmesan Cheese; 66
Avocado Chocolate Mousse; 75
Avocado Shrimp Salad Lettuce Wraps; 30
Avocado Toast with Poached Eggs; 25
Baked Apples with Cinnamon; 85
Baked Apples with Cinnamon and Walnuts; 73
Baked Cod with Lemon and Herbs; 60
Baked Cod with Roasted Vegetables; 50
Baked Egg Cups with Spinach and Tomato; 24
Baked Lemon Pepper Mahi Mahi; 62
Baked Pear Crisp with Oat Topping; 71
Baked Sweet Potato Fries with Yogurt Dip; 28
Baked Tilapia with Tomato and Herb Relish; 57
Banana Chips; 37
Beetroot and Feta Bruschetta; 31
Berry Tart with Almond Flour Crust; 74
Black Bean and Sweet Potato Chili; 77
Breakfast Quinoa Bowl with Mixed Fruit; 21
Broiled Scallops with Garlic Butter; 57
Brown Rice with Peas and Carrots; 66
Caprese Skewers with Cherry Tomatoes, Mozzarella, and Basil; 28
Carrot Sticks with Hummus; 36
Cauliflower Fried Rice with Tofu; 42
Chia Seed Pudding with Fresh Fruit Topping; 34
Chicken and Vegetable Paella; 78
Chicken Piccata with Whole Wheat Pasta; 53
Coconut Curry Shrimp with Rice Noodles; 61
Coconut Milk Rice Pudding with Mango; 72
Cottage Cheese with Pineapple Chunks; 37
Crispy Eggplant Parmesan; 86
Cucumber and Hummus Bites; 27
Cucumber and Smoked Salmon Roll-Ups; 49
Dark Chocolate Covered Strawberries; 73
Deviled Eggs with Greek Yogurt and Dill; 29
Egg White Frittata with Spinach, Mushrooms, and Feta; 21
Eggplant Caponata; 65
Frozen Banana Bites with Peanut Butter; 75
Fruit Salad with Cottage Cheese; 24
Fruit Salsa with Cinnamon Pita Chips; 30
Garlic Roasted Green Beans; 68
Greek Yogurt Dip with Fresh Veggies; 31
Greek Yogurt Parfait with Fresh Berries and Almonds; 22
Grilled Corn on the Cob with Lime Cilantro Butter; 68
Grilled Eggplant Rolls with Quinoa and Pesto; 27
Grilled Lobster with Herb Butter; 59
Grilled Pineapple with Honey and Mint; 70
Grilled Shrimp Skewers with Pineapple and Bell Pepper; 49
Grilled Steak Salad with Balsamic Vinaigrette; 53
Grilled Swordfish with Mango Salsa; 59
Grilled Zucchini Rolls with Herbed Goat Cheese; 32
Harissa Spiced Chicken Thighs; 83
Homemade Granola Bars with Oats, Nuts, and Dried Fruit; 34
Lemon Garlic Chicken Skewers; 52
Lemon Herb Baked Cod Fillets; 45
Lemon Herb Tilapia; 62
Lemon Poppy Seed Muffins with Whole Wheat Flour; 70
Lentil and Vegetable Curry; 79
Lentil Soup with Vegetables; 40
Mango Sorbet; 72
Mediterranean Quinoa Salad; 80
Minestrone Soup with Whole Wheat Pasta; 41
Oatmeal with Banana and Walnuts; 23
Pan-Seared Duck Breast with Orange Glaze; 54
Pan-Seared Sea Bass with Lemon Caper Sauce; 60
Pork Stir-Fry with Snow Peas and Water Chestnuts; 55
Potato Leek Gratin with Gruyere Cheese; 67
Quinoa and Black Bean Stuffed Peppers; 81
Quinoa Breakfast Bowl with Sautéed Vegetables and Egg; 25

Quinoa Pilaf with Vegetables; 65
Quinoa Salad Jars with Veggies and Lemon Herb Dressing; 36
Ratatouille Stuffed Bell Peppers; 84
Ratatouille with Chickpeas; 79
Roasted Brussels Sprouts with Balsamic Glaze; 84
Salmon and Quinoa Salad with Lemon-Dill Dressing; 46
Sautéed Spinach with Garlic and Lemon; 67
Seafood Paella with Brown Rice; 46
Seafood Paella with Shrimp, Mussels, and Clams; 58
Seafood Risotto with Asparagus and Peas; 47
Seafood Salad with Greek Yogurt Dressing; 48
Seared Scallops with White Wine Sauce; 63
Seaweed Salad with Sesame Dressing; 35
Shrimp and Vegetable Stir-Fry with Brown Rice; 49
Spaghetti Squash with Marinara Sauce; 41
Spinach Salad with Strawberries and Almonds; 39
Steel-Cut Oats with Apple Cinnamon Compote; 23
Stuffed Acorn Squash with Quinoa and Cranberries; 77
Stuffed Bell Peppers with Quinoa and Black Beans; 87
Stuffed Portobello Mushrooms with Quinoa and Spinach; 43
Stuffed Squid with Quinoa and Spinach; 45
Thai Coconut Curry Mussels; 48
Tofu Satay Skewers with Peanut Sauce; 29
Tomato Basil Bruschetta; 42
Trail Mix with Nuts, Seeds, and Dried Fruit; 36
Turkey Chili with Beans and Corn; 52
Vegan Sushi Rolls with Avocado and Cucumber; 35
Vegetable and Bean Chili; 40
Whole Grain Pancakes with Blueberry Compote; 22
Whole Wheat Pasta Primavera with Roasted Vegetables; 39
Zucchini Chips with Herbed Yogurt Dip; 85

Made in the USA
Las Vegas, NV
19 February 2025

18388822R00063